ARUNDEL CASTLE

SOLA VIRTUS INVICTA

ARUNDEL CASTLE

A seat of The Duke of Norfolk E.M.

A short history and guide by

John Martin Robinson
Maltravers Herald of Arms

Phillimore

1994

Published by
PHILLIMORE & CO. LTD.
Shopwyke Manor Barn, Chichester, Sussex

ISBN 0 85033 904 9

Printed in Great Britain by
CHICHESTER PRESS LTD.

Contents

Acknowledgements

I wish to thank the following for help in the preparation of this book:

The Duke of Norfolk

Mrs Ian Rodger (who assisted with the research)

Mrs Colin Wallace (who typed the manuscript)

The Royal Commission on the Historical Monuments of England for allowing their survey photographs of the Castle by Sid Barker and James O. Davies to be published here for the first time, and Stephen Croad for organising this survey. The following illustrations are reproduced by permission of RCHME: 6-8, 21, 46, 48, 50-6, 59-69, 72, 76, 77, 83, 88-90, 93-7, 99-101, 103, 108-115, 118-124, 126

No.42 is reproduced by permission of Apertures of Arundel

No.104 is reproduced by permission of Mrs de Lazlo

All other illustrations are the copyright of His Grace The Duke of Norfolk.

JOHN MARTIN ROBINSON
May 1994

Foreword

It is often assumed that Arundel Castle is almost entirely a Victorian reconstruction. In fact it is two things in one, as is recognised by its status as both a scheduled ancient monument and a Grade I listed building. It is a great Norman and medieval castle, of which as much, or more, survives as in many of the ruined castles which are thought to be more 'genuine'. It has a largely intact series of massive 11th-century earthworks, including an impressive motte and extensive outer system of banks and ditches, a stone gatehouse dating from 1070, a complete curtain wall (apart from one small section in the south-west corner) constructed between the late 11th and late 12th century, a perfect shell keep erected in 1140, and a very well-preserved barbican of *c*.1300. Within this fortified framework, occupying the site of the medieval domestic quarters in the south bailey, is the largest inhabited Victorian Gothic Revival house in England, which dates mainly from between 1875 and 1900. It is this, with its dramatic skyline, which gives Arundel its dominant 19th-century character, but even this great Victorian pile incorporates both the two-storeyed shell and vaulted undercroft of a palace built by King Henry II in around 1180 and the library constructed by the 11th Duke and his team of Cumberland craftsmen in 1800, which is one of the most original and best-preserved late-Georgian Gothick interiors. Arundel is also one of the longest inhabited country houses in England, the Dukes of Norfolk and their ancestors through the female line having lived here for over eight hundred and fifty years, since 1138. This long history is explained in more detail in the following pages.

ALBINI

WILLIAM de ALBINI, 1st Earl of Arundel—ADELIZA of Louvain, widow of Henry I (d.1176)

WILLIAM, 2nd Earl of Arundel (d.1193)—Maud de St HILAIRE du HARCOUET

WILLIAM, 3rd Earl of Arundel (d.1221)—MABEL LE MESCHIN

WILLIAM, 4th Earl of Arundel (d.1224)   HUGH, 5th Earl of Arundel (d.1243)   ISABEL—JOHN FITZALAN, Lord of Clun and C

JOHN FITZALAN of Arundel (d.1267)—MAUD

FITZALAN

JOHN FITZALAN of Arundel (d.1272)—ISABEL

RICHARD FITZALAN, 1st Earl of Arundel (d.1302)—ALICE of Saluzzo

EDMUND, 2nd Earl of Arundel (d.1326)—ALICE de WARENNE

RICHARD, 3rd Earl of Arundel (d.1376)—(2) ELEANOR of Lancaster, niece of Edward I

RICHARD, 4th Earl of Arundel (beheaded 1397)—ELIZABETH BOHUN   JOHN, Lord Arundel (drowned 1379)—ELEA

THOMAS, 5th Earl of Arundel (d.1415)   ELIZABETH—(2) THOMAS MOWBRAY   JOHN FITZALAN—ELIZABETH DESPEN(
Duke of Norfolk (opposite)   (or Arundel) (d.1390)

JOHN, 6th Earl of Arundel (d.1421)—ELEAN

JOHN, 7th Earl of Arundel (d.1435)—(2) MAUD LOVELL   WILLIAM, 9th Earl of Arundel (d.1487)—LA

HUMPHREY, 8th Earl of Arundel (d.1483, aged 9)   THOMAS, 10th Earl of Arundel (d.1524)—M

WILLIAM, 11th Earl of Arundel (d.1544)—(2) ANNE PERCY

HENRY, 12th Earl of Arundel (d.1580)—(1) CATHERINE GREY

LADY MARY FITZALAN (1) (d.1557)—THOMAS HOWARD, 4th Duke of Norfolk★ (beheaded 1572)

PHILIP, 13th Earl of Arundel (d.1595)—ANNE DACRE

THOMAS, 14th Earl of Arundel★ also Earl of Surrey and Norfolk (d.1646)—LADY ALETHEIA TALBOT

HENRY FREDERICK, 15th Earl of Arundel—LADY ELIZABETH STUART
also Earl of Surrey and Norfolk (d.1652)

THOMAS, 5th Duke of Norfolk (d.1677)   HENRY, 6th Duke of Norfolk★ (d.1684)—(1) LADY ANNE SOMERSET   LOR

HENRY, 7th Duke of Norfolk★ (d.1701)   LORD THOMAS HOWARD (d.1689)—MARY ELIZABETH SAVILLE   HEN

THOMAS, 8th Duke of Norfolk★ (d.1732)   EDWARD, 9th Duke of Norfolk★ (d.1777)   CHA

CHARLES, 11th Duke of Norfolk★ (d.1815)   BERNARD, 12th Duke of Norfolk★ (d.1852)—LADY ELIZABETH BELASYSE

HENRY CHARLES, 13th Duke of Norfolk★ (d.1856)—LADY CHARLOTTE SOPHIA LEVESON-GOWER

HENRY GRANVILLE FITAZALAN-HOWARD—HON. AUGUSTA LYONS   EDWARD GEOR
14th Duke of Norfolk★ (d.1860)   2nd son created Lord Howard of Glossop, 1869 (d.1883)

HENRY, 15th Duke of Norfolk★ (d.1917)—(2) GWENDOLINE MARY CONSTABLE-MAXWELL, Lady Herries   FRA
2nd Lord Howard o

BERNARD MARMADUKE, 16th Duke of Norfolk★ (d.1975)—HON. LAVINIA MARY STRUTT   BER
3rd Lord Howard of

LADY HERRIES   LADY MARY   LADY SARAH   LADY JANE   MIL
12th Baron B

EDWARD WILLIAM—GEORGINA GORE   LORD GERALD BERNARD   LADY TESSA MARY ISABEL
Earl of Arundel

HENRY MILES, Lord Maltravers   HON. THOMAS   LADY RACHEL ROSE

★indicates Marshal or Earl Marshal of England

Pedigree of the
Fitzalan and Howard Families

ER

IMER

HOWARD

EDWARD I, King of England 1272-1307┬(2) MARGARET of Valois

THOMAS of Brotherton, Earl of Norfolk★ (d.1338)┬(1) ALICE de HALES

MARGARET, Duchess of Norfolk (d.1399)┬(1) JOHN, 4th Lord Segrave

TRAVERS

ELIZABETH SEGRAVE┬JOHN, 4th Lord Mowbray (d.1368)

THOMAS MOWBRAY, 1st Duke of Norfolk★ (d.1399)┬(2) ELIZABETH FITZALAN (opposite)

ELEY

LADY MARGARET MOWBRAY┬SIR ROBERT HOWARD

NEVILL

JOHN HOWARD, 1st Duke of Norfolk★ (k.1485)┬(1) CATHERINE de MOLEYNS

WIDVILE

THOMAS, 2nd Duke of Norfolk★ (d.1524)┬(1) ELIZABETH TYLNEY

THOMAS, 3rd Duke of Norfolk★ (d.1554)┬(2) LADY ELIZABETH STAFFORD

HENRY, Earl of Surrey (beheaded 1547)┬LADY FRANCES VERE

ES HOWARD (d.1713)┬MARY TATTERSHALL

LES HOWARD (d.1720)┬MARY AYLWARD

Duke of Norfolk★ (d.1786)┬KATHERINE BROCKHOLES

LORD BERNARD HOWARD (d.1717)┬CATHERINE TATTERSHALL

BERNARD HOWARD (d.1735)┬HON ANNE ROPER

HENRY HOWARD (d.1787)┬JULIANA MOLYNEUX

LAN-HOWARD┬(1) AUGUSTA TALBOT

WARD┬(1) CLARA LOUISA GREENWOOD
.1924)

WARD┬MONA JOSEPHINE TEMPEST STAPLETON, BARONESS BEAUMONT (d.1971)
1972)

S, 17th Duke of Norfolk★┬ANNE MARY TERESA CONSTABLE MAXWELL
h Lord Howard of Glossop

LADY CARINA MARY GABRIEL   LADY MARCIA MARY JOSEPHINE

LADY ISABEL

'An old English family mansion is a fertile subject for study.
It abounds with illustrations of former times and traces of the tastes,
and humours and manners of successive generations.'

Washington Irving

Chapter I
The Middle Ages

Arundel Castle was founded on Christmas Day 1067. It is possible to be precise. William Duke of Normandy, the year following his conquest of England, held his Christmas Court at Gloucester. There the new King of England rewarded his most important and loyal supporters and followers for their contribution to his success. These included his kinsman, Roger de Montgomery, who was one of the half-dozen cronies that William felt he could really trust.

Montgomery had been left behind in Normandy during the Battle of Hastings, to protect William's interests there and to ensure that nothing untoward happened while the ruler was out of the country. As a reward for his services Roger was granted large tracts of land on the Welsh Marches and in Shropshire, and also a third of the county of Sussex. The latter came with the condition that he should build a castle near the mouth of the River Arun to protect the gap formed by the river valley through the natural defences of the South Downs.

The Conqueror divided much of Sussex among his most reliable henchmen. In return for their landholdings they were obliged to build and maintain castles forming a chain of coastal defences intended to deter others from attempting what William himself had just successfully achieved by crossing the Channel and invading England. These feudal castleries were Arundel, Bramber, Lewes, Pevensey and Hastings, with the royal castles of Dover in Kent and Carisbrooke on the Isle of Wight holding either flank.

There has long been debate as to whether there were any pre-Conquest defences on the present site of Arundel Castle. There was certainly some kind of ancient settlement in the area, and Roman tiles for instance, have been found in the Little Park to the north of the castle. It seems most likely, however, that Roger de Montgomery was the first to fortify the present site. The entry in Domesday Book, which Victorian antiquarians took as evidence for a pre-existing castle at Arundel, is ambiguous. The older defensive works protecting the valley were on the opposite side of the river at Warningcamp, where ancient earthworks still exist.

Roger de Montgomery immediately erected a motte and bailey castle of timber and earth on his new Sussex estate. His castle was planned with a central motte between two baileys, rather than the single bailey more usually encountered in Norman castles. But his was not an entirely unusual layout. Windsor is today the largest and best-known example in England, while Carisbrooke, Rockingham and Alnwick are others; and there are several castles of similar double-bailey plan in Normandy itself, such as Grimboscai south of Caen.

The earthworks at Arundel, begun in 1068, are very impressive and survive in good condition. They consist of the central motte (a large flat-topped cone) protected by a deep fosse or dry ditch on the west side. The motte is 100 ft. high from the bottom of the ditch, and 69 ft. high on its inner side. The total dimensions of the castle, from north to south, are 950 ft., and the baileys are approximately 250 ft. across. The motte and baileys form the nucleus of a larger defensive area which includes extensive outer earthworks on the vulnerable landward side to the north west, including a double fosse and high embankments which encircle the whole of the Little Park, now the castle cricket ground.

The original temporary timber defences were gradually replaced with masonry in the course of the succeeding hundred years, beginning with the main entrance to the castle, the gatehouse into the south bailey, and sections of the encircling curtain wall. There was no stone around Arundel itself, so much of the building material for the castle had to be brought from a distance by water transport. The gatehouse, which was constructed *c.*1070, is of Pulborough stone in roughly squared ashlar blocks, carried down river for fifteen miles by boat. Similar stonework can also be found in the curtain wall though this is largely constructed of flint in a

1 Arundel Castle from the east showing the Victorian skyline and 12th-century fabric.

herringbone pattern; the flints, of course, being easily obtained from the surrounding chalk downs. The gatehouse retains its original rectangular portcullis groove, similar to that in Arques-la-Bataille, the well-known castle near Dieppe in Normandy.

Roger de Montgomery died in 1094 and was succeeded at Arundel by his eldest son Robert, known as Robert de Bellême and characterised by contemporary chroniclers as cruel and keen on military architecture. He rebelled against Henry I who punished him for his disloyalty. In Robert's absence, Arundel was besieged. After a campaign of three months the castle surrendered and Robert was banished for life; his lands and the castle were confiscated by the Crown.

Between 1102 and the 1130s Arundel was in the possession of Henry I, but under the terms of the king's will it was re-granted to his second wife Adeliza of Louvain as her dower. Three years after the king's death, in 1138 she re-married William d'Albini II, son of William d'Albini I of Buckenham in Norfolk, Chief Butler to William the Conqueror. His grand marriage went to his head and, according to a contemporary chronicler, d'Albini became 'so puffed up that he looked down on every man except the King'. It can be said that, apart from the occasional reversion to the Crown, Arundel has descended directly from 1138 to the present day, carried by female heiresses from the d'Albinis to the Fitzalans in the 13th century and then from the Fitzalans to the Howards in the 16th century.

William d'Albini II, who was made Earl of Sussex, was a great builder and responsible for erecting the castle of New Buckenham, to replace his father's at Old Buckenham, as well as the large

2 View of the Norman keep and gatehouse, before restoration, painted by James Canter, c.1770.

square keep at Castle Rising on his Norfolk estates. At Arundel he built the stone shell keep on top of Roger de Montgomery's post-Conquest motte. He began it almost immediately after his marriage to Adeliza in 1138. It is finely constructed of Caen stone, brought across the sea from Normandy, and Quarr Abbey stone from the Isle of Wight. It is an irregular oval in plan, perpetuating in solid masonry the form of the post-Conquest timber palisade which it replaced. The walls are approximately 10 ft. thick and 27 ft. high. The diameter of the keep is 59 ft. in one direction and 67 ft. in the other. The exterior is smooth and severe, punctuated at intervals by shallow buttresses.

It relies for its effect on the quality of the ashlar stonework and a single spectacular architectural feature, a large entrance archway (now blocked) on the south side. This would originally have been approached by a straight flight of steps up the motte from the south bailey. The external face of this archway is richly carved with characteristic Norman embellishment: roll mouldings and chevron ornaments which are almost identical to the decoration of the arches in the keep at Castle Hedingham in Essex, the contemporary seat of the De Veres.

In William d'Albini's day the rest of the castle was still partly of timber. The baileys must be

3 The Keep built c.1140 and motte c.1068.

imagined, therefore, lined with lean-to wooden structures, stables for horses, stores for provisions and barracks for soldiers and servants, while some of the open space within the walls was a garden, growing herbs, vegetables, medicinal plants and flowers. Presiding over this from the summit of the motte the new keep with its sleek and sophisticated exterior was the home of the earl himself, and a powerful statement of his rank. Inside its defensive shell it contained his own residential accommodation including a hall, lit from an internal courtyard, as well as a chapel dedicated to St Martin.

The d'Albini family, like the Montgomerys before them, had a special devotion to St Martin, the patron saint of soldiers (who gave half his cloak to a beggar). William d'Albini I, father of the 1st Earl, was the benefactor of the Abbey of St Martin d'Aubigny at Lessaye in Normandy, while the Benedictine monks in the priory at Arundel, established by Roger de Montgomery, came from the Abbey of Séez in Normandy which was also dedicated to St Martin.

By the mid-12th century, the castle of a tenant-in-chief, like Arundel, had become at least as much the house of its owner and the administrative headquarters of his fief, as a military defence. The greatest Norman land-holdings, those of the tenants-in-chief, who held their estates directly from the king (including abbots and bishops as well as earls and barons), were known as Honours. An honour covered many square miles, but was as much a system of customary dues as a geographic unit. It comprised many kinds of labour services, fiscal levies and the profits of justice, as well as the demesne farm, forests and parks of its lord. All this required an efficient organisation to administer. The 'capital' of an honour usually comprised a burgh or town established in the shadow of the castle and provided with various commercial privileges and religious foundations under the patronage of its lord, and this was the case at Arundel where the town had a port and market, and a Benedictine priory founded by Roger de Montgomery.

By the standards of the time, the interior of the keep would have been luxurious, as the richly decorated doorway still demonstrates. Mid-12th-century Arundel should be thought of, not so much as an austere military establishment, but as a complex and sophisticated place with the keep a fit residence for a queen-dowager and her ambitious second husband, and the hub of a far-spreading fiscal, administrative and judicial system dealing with the practical problems of this world, while the elaborate Cluniac liturgy of the Benedictine monks from St Martin at Séez in the various chapels prepared the way for the next.

There is very little contemporary evidence to record the appearance of Norman Arundel. So its atmosphere can perhaps best be captured by quoting from Romantic 19th century literature, such as the description of a Norman castle in Flaubert's Legend of St Julian Hospitaller (1877) which like much of Flaubert's writing was based on serious historical research:

Julian's father and mother lived in a castle in the middle of a forest on the slope of a hill ... The pavement of the courtyard was as clean as the flagstones of a church. The long gutter-spouts shaped like dragons hanging head-down spat all the rain water into a cistern; and on every window sill of every storey a basil or heliotrope flowered in a painted earthenware pot ... Inside the castle the ironwork shone brightly everywhere; tapestries lined the walls to keep out the cold; and the cupboards were crammed with linen, the cellars piled high with tuns of wine, and the oak coffers creaking under the weight of money bags.

4 Norman curtain wall and Gatehouse built c.1070.

5 *Curtain wall round north bailey before restoration.*

In the armoury, between military standards and wild beasts' heads were to be seen weapons of every age and every nation from Amalekite slings and Garamantian javelins to Saracen brackmards and Norman coats of mail.

The master-spit in the kitchen could roast an ox. The chapel was as magnificent as a king's oratory.

The only well-documented incident at Arundel in the lifetime of Adeliza and William d'Albini was the visit there in 1139 of the Empress Matilda, daughter of Henry I, on her arrival in England to press her claim to the throne against Stephen. She stayed at the castle for some time, but when Stephen threatened to besiege Arundel, a safe-conduct to Bristol was negotiated for her and she left peacefully. Thereafter William d'Albini did not take sides in the struggle between Stephen and Matilda, which was finally decided in favour of Matilda's son who succeeded on Stephen's death as Henry II, King of England, Duke of Normandy and Count of Anjou.

When Adeliza died in 1151 Henry II gave a charter to William d'Albini confirming him in the earldom, castle and honour of Arundel for life. He

in turn died in 1176, and according to the Norman law of dôt, whereby the dowry of a mother did not automatically descend to her children, the castle reverted into the hands of the Crown, which retained it from 1178 to 1189. Henry II stayed at the castle in 1182 and probably on other occasions, and carried out various architectural works. The Pipe Rolls (in the Public Record Office) record moneys spent by Henry II 'in work upon the Castle of Arundel', 'in work upon the houses within the Castle of Arundel', 'in work upon the great tower', 'in work upon the Herbarium [herb garden] before the King's great chamber', and also a chapel. The cost of these works totalled over £339 (compared, for example, to £100 spent on the castle at Canterbury, £150 at Rochester, £347 at Southampton and £428 at Chilham). Castle building under Henry II, as under his successors Richard and John, was the largest single item of royal expenditure.

Henry II converted the royal castles at Windsor and Winchester into palaces, and at Arundel, while it was in his hands, the aim was to improve the

6 *Undercroft in Henry II range built c.1180.*

domestic amenities rather than to strengthen the defences. In place of William d'Albini's somewhat constricted house within the keep, Henry II built a new domestic range on the south side of the south bailey, which remains the nucleus of the house at Arundel today; a surprising amount of Henry's work having survived later reconstructions. The new royal house contained a great hall and king's chamber in a range 25 ft. wide, raised over a vaulted undercroft. The chapel at the west end of this range projected beyond the line of the curtain wall which it is also likely was completed in stone along the east side of the south bailey at this time. Henry II's house survives two storeys high in the present south wing of the castle. The vaulted undercroft is intact, 60 ft. long with double splayed windows now opening into the lower passage, though originally they faced the south bailey. The upper walls of Henry II's building form the shell of the present drawing-room while his chapel (dedicated to St

George, and which remained in use till 1789), now reconstructed and enlarged out of recognition, is the principal dining-room of the present house.

The most impressive survival of Henry II's time, however, is the pair of blocked two light windows in the outer wall of the drawing-room, which are beautiful late 12th-century work, almost identical to windows at Winchester or in the keep at Pembroke Castle. The herb garden outside the king's bedroom window, referred to in the Pipe Roll, is possibly the square garden surrounded by embankments, below the south front, now called the bowling green. If this is Henry II's 'herbarium', it makes it the oldest surviving garden in England.

In view of his construction of an elegant and comfortable new house at Arundel, it is clear that Henry II intended to hold on to the castle, but in the event it was returned to the d'Albini family, in the person of William d'Albini III who in 1190 recovered the Honour of Arundel from King

7 Doorway in Henry II range.

8 Window in Henry II range.

Richard I (who had visited the castle the previous year), on payment of 2,000 marks. The following year he paid another fine for the castle. Similar fines were paid to the Crown for seizin of the castle and honour of Arundel by all the succeeding d'Albini earls. (Contrary to the assumption of many commentators, death or succession duties are not a uniquely modern phenomenon.) The 2nd Earl's son, also William, paid to have the castle in 1198. William d'Albini IV, 3rd Earl, died near Rome in 1221 en route for the Holy Land. He was succeeded by both his sons in turn, neither of whom had male heirs, William V (who died in 1224) and Hugh who succeeded while still a minor. On his death in 1243 the male line of the d'Albinis came to an end.

The castle and honour of Arundel then devolved on his nephew John Fitzalan (whose father, also John, Lord of Clun and Oswestry in Shropshire had married Isabel d'Albini, the sister of William V and Hugh). The Fitzalans, like the Montgomerys and the d'Albinis, had come to England from France after the Norman Conquest; they originated in Brittany and share a common ancestry with the Scottish Stuarts. Neither John Fitzalan nor his son, another John, was styled Earl of Arundel, perhaps because Hugh d'Albini's widow was still alive. She outlived her husband for nearly forty years and had a substantial dowry out of the d'Albini lands.

On the death of the younger John Fitzalan in 1272 Arundel passed to his five-year-old son Richard who was created Earl of Arundel (the first of his line) in 1289. Four years earlier Richard had been granted by King Edward I the right to hold two fairs a year at Arundel and to tax the commodities sold there. This additional source of revenue provided the cash for further building work at the castle which must by that stage have been rather old-fashioned, if not dilapidated, after the various minorities and the long period in dower for Hugh d'Albini's widow.

Richard, Earl of Arundel was close to Edward I and fought with him in Scotland. He is described in the Roll of the Siege of Caerlaverock in 1300: 'A handsome and well-loved knight, I saw there richly armed In red with gold lion rampant' (a reference to his surcoat displaying the Fitzalan arms of a gold lion on a red ground).

Richard's wife Alicia, daughter of the Marquis of Saluzzo in Piedmont, was a kinswoman of

Edward I through his mother Eleanor of Provence. Being connected to the king, Richard was in a position to know at first hand Edward's great castle-building programme in Wales and this provided the source of inspiration for his own improvements at Arundel, where he completed the curtain wall, reconstructed the north bailey postern gate (north-west of the keep) to form what is now called Bevis' Tower. This displays the shouldered Caernarvon windows which are a feature of Richard Fitzalan's work at Arundel. He also reconstructed the entrance to the keep and built the Well Tower, next to the 12th-century St Martin's Tower. His best-preserved addition to the castle, however, was a new barbican with two square towers in front of the Norman gateway which he also heightened. This, like all Richard Fitzalan's work at the castle, is built of knapped flint with dressings of Pulborough stone, and has the characteristic Caernarvon windows.

As well as providing an additional defence before the entrance to the castle, the barbican also contained lodgings for the Earl's principal retainers, possibly his chaplain and the constable of the castle. (A constable is recorded continuously at Arundel from 1244 to 1589.) Each of the two upper floors is planned as a self-contained flat with a large central hall flanked by two smaller chambers and a garderobe. These rooms are the best-preserved medieval interiors at Arundel and give a good idea of the type of accommodation enjoyed by what might be called the 'upper-middle' ranks of society in the late 13th century.

Richard, the 1st Fitzalan Earl of Arundel, died aged only 35 in 1302. His son Edmund, 2nd Earl, found himself caught up in the struggles between Edward II and the latter's ghastly queen, Isabella 'the She-wolf of France'. Edmund Fitzalan was captured by Isabella's lover, Mortimer, who beheaded him without trial at Hereford in 1326, and Arundel Castle once more reverted to the Crown. It was granted briefly to the King's half-brother Edmund, Earl of Kent but he in turn was executed in 1330 and the following year the castle, honour and Earldom of Arundel were restored to Edmund Fitzalan's son, another Richard.

Richard, 3rd Earl of Arundel was in many ways the most interesting of the medieval Fitzalans. From his maternal uncle John de Warenne he inherited very large estates and the Earldom of Surrey, in addition to the Fitzalan patrimony. He used his financial capital well, as the basis for a

banking business, lending money to the king or London merchants for a profit. (The Church's laws against usury in the Middle Ages were got round, not by charging interest as such but by lending money on fixed term contracts; if the sum was not repaid on time then the lender was entitled to double that which had originally been lent.) As a result of his inheritances and his own endeavours, the 3rd Earl became the richest man in England in the mid-14th century. In his will he left 90,359 marks in hard cash, half of which was stored in the keep at Arundel which he used as his treasury. Like a modern tycoon he also spent lavishly. When his younger son Thomas (who later became Archbishop of Canterbury) was studying at Oriel College, Oxford, the 3rd Earl built a new chapel there at his own expense.

He made Arundel his principal home continuing the works of enlargement begun by his grandfather. He built a new range on the west side of the south bailey incorporating a large great hall rising the full height of the castle with a steep pitched roof. This hall, which was again substantially remodelled in the 15th century, was (apart from the keep) the dominant architectural feature of the castle in the later Middle Ages. Hollar's engraving of Arundel in 1643 shows its roof riding high above the surrounding buildings and the curtain wall. It must have had a magnificent interior but not much is known about it except that it had an elaborate, open, timber roof which one commentator compared with Westminster Hall. In the space between the new hall and the gatehouse was a range of chambers with the kitchen, buttery, pantry and other domestic offices. The 3rd Earl converted the south range into private rooms for the family and important visitors, Henry II's old great hall being divided into chambers. The narrow wing backing on to the curtain wall along the east side of the courtyard was reconstructed as lodgings for the many retainers in the castle. As well as a small army of domestic servants the 3rd Earl's household included a constable, warder, porter, chaplains, usher of the chamber, treasurer, comptroller, yeoman of the wardrobe and marshal of the household, and like that of all great noblemen at the time was a smaller-scale echo of the royal household. All these 'headmen' required substantial accommodation of their own.

The 3rd Earl's son, also Richard, the 4th Earl of Arundel continued his father's work of improvement and lived at Arundel in the same great state. The wedding of his younger daughter in 1384 was attended by King Richard II, the Queen and many of the leading nobles, with a great feast in the new great hall. The 4th Earl's principal architectural achievement at Arundel, however, was not secular but ecclesiastical. His father in 1354 had obtained a papal bull to enlarge the perpetual chantry he had founded in 1344, to form a college of 12 priests under the rule of a Master. This had not progressed very far at the time of the 3rd Earl's death in 1376. His son 'eagerly embraced the interests of the intended establishment'.

The little Benedictine priory at Arundel had begun to decay and the attached parochial church was in poor condition; it seemed to the 4th Earl that the best plan would be to rebuild that church as the intended collegiate foundation rather than having it within the castle itself (as is the case, for instance, at Windsor). He consequently petitioned Richard II to dissolve the priory and attach its revenues to the new college. He undertook to provide a new church and conventual buildings, to increase the number of clergy to 13 and to dedicate the whole as a college of secular canons 'in honour of the Blessed Trinity, of the Blessed Virgin Mary, and of all the saints'. The foundation of the College was secured by a patent dated 1 April 1380 and the first buildings were ready for occupation by 1381, though work on the church itself continued for several more years.

It was characteristic of the later Middle Ages that the earl should have founded a secular college with a chantry function. By that date the interest of pious benefactors had moved away from monastic foundations, in remote areas, to what were thought of as more serviceable religious institutions in towns. The 4th Earl's new college was a tripartite foundation. It comprised a parish church for the townspeople of Arundel in the nave and transepts (dedicated like its predecessor to St Nicholas), flanked to the east (and separated from the rest of the church by a contemporary iron grille) by the collegiate chantry chapel occupying the chancel, and now known as the Fitzalan Chapel. This was richly furnished with carved oak choir stalls (very similar to the contemporary ones at New College, Oxford), magnificent jewelled plate and finely embroidered vestments (including altar frontals with Fitzalan heraldry) all given by the earl.

The new chapel formed the setting for a splendid daily liturgy with a choir of boys and men (like a cathedral or university college), and for the next hundred years or so Arundel was an important centre of music, noted for its early polyphony as well as Gregorian chant. (Some of the parchment sheets with musical settings for the liturgy survive re-used on the back as account books.)

Accommodation for the 12 priests and a house for the Master were provided in a two-storeyed quadrangle to the south east of the chancel, which still survives though much repaired and altered. The third part of the foundation was a Maison Dieu or almshouse for the old and infirm which occupied a further (probably single-storeyed) quadrangle to the west of the parish church. This has almost disappeared apart from stretches of masonry and an arched doorway now incorporated in the wall round the castle car park and kitchen garden. (Its function, however, continues today as the old college buildings have been converted to almshouses under the aegis of the Order of Malta.)

The 4th Earl, himself, like his grandfather before him came to a sticky end. Though he had carried the crown at the coronation of Richard II and been in favour at Court in the early years of the reign, he later fell out with the king and became one of his leading political opponents. Despite receiving a pardon from the king for alleged political offences, he was nonetheless treacherously seized in the City of London, tried for treason and beheaded in Cheapside in 1397 'no more shrinking or changing colour than if he were going to a banquet'. Because of his sudden end he was not buried in his new chapel at Arundel. The castle once more reverted to the Crown and was granted by Richard II to John Holland, Duke of Exeter. But when Henry IV seized the throne Holland was executed and in 1400 Richard Fitzalan's son Thomas was restored as 5th Earl of Arundel and received back the castle. He was the first member of the family to be buried in the new chapel, and his fine tomb of carved alabaster occupies a place of honour in front of the high altar with effigies of himself and his wife Beatrice, daughter of King John I of Portugal. (Her Portuguese lady-in-waiting, Mistress Salmon is also commemorated nearby in a finely engraved brass.)

The 5th Earl of Arundel played a prominent part in the Hundred Years' War fighting with

*9 (left)   The Fitzalan Chapel built by the 4th Earl of Arundel,
1380, under the terms of his father's will.*

*10 (above)   Effigies of the 5th Earl and his wife Beatrice of
Portugal.*

Henry V. He died of dysentery contracted at the
siege of Harfleur in 1415. He had no son and was
succeeded at Arundel by his cousin Lord Maltravers
(a barony in fee inherited through his mother).
The Warenne inheritance, however, passed to the
Mowbrays as a result of the 5th Earl's sister Elizabeth's marriage to Thomas Mowbray, Duke of
Norfolk. The 15th-century Earls of Arundel were
not as rich as their predecessors had been and, as a
result, seem to have spent less on architectural
improvements to the castle. They continued to play
a part in the Hundred Years' War. John, 7th Earl
was nicknamed the 'English Achilles'; over six feet
tall, he was a distinguished soldier. As a reward for
his services in France he was created Duke of
Touraine by the Regent Bedford in 1434. He died
after having his leg amputated at Beauvais in the
following year. He was brought back and buried at

Arundel (minus his leg) in the Fitzalan Chapel
where both he and his father have impressive tombs,
his father's of Purbeck with enamelled brass
decorations and his own with a carved and coloured
effigy on top and a stark cadaver underneath as a
memento mori.

His baby son Humphrey, who succeeded as
8th Earl, died aged nine in 1438 and the honour
and castle then passed to Humphrey's uncle William
who became 9th Earl of Arundel. He married
Beatrice Nevile, the sister of 'Warwick the King-
Maker'. They too have an impressive tomb in the
Fitzalan Chapel with beautifully carved and painted
effigies of Caen stone set in a Purbeck marble
chantry of almost oriental elaboration. He is best
remembered as the patron of William Caxton, the
printer, whose edition of the Golden Legend is
dedicated to him. His son Thomas, 10th Earl, and

11 *Tomb of the 7th Earl of Arundel.*

William, 11th Earl continued the illustrious traditions of the Fitzalans. The 10th Earl married Margaret Woodville, sister of Edward IV's queen, and later was godfather to Prince Arthur, the elder son of Henry VII. The 11th Earl was a confidant of Henry VIII and supported his divorce from Catherine of Aragon.

In return Henry VIII acted as godfather to his eldest son, who was called Henry after the king, and succeeded his father as 12th Earl of Arundel in 1544. In his early life Henry played an active role in public affairs, taking part in the siege of Boulogne in 1544, acting as Lord High Constable at the coronation of Edward VI, serving as Governor of Calais. At one stage it was rumoured that he would marry Princess Elizabeth, but this came to nothing, and in fact his strong Catholicism led to his gradual withdrawal from public life as Elizabeth's reign progressed. In 1564 he resigned all his offices and retired to his estates where he formed a great library and was a generous patron of music. The Tallis 40-part motet is reputed to have been commissioned

12 *12th and last Fitzalan Earl of Arundel by John Bettes I.*

13   *Tomb of the 10th, 11th and 12th Earls of Arundel, 1595*
in the Fitzalan Chapel.

by the Earl of Arundel to show foreign musicians what English composers could do. It was first performed at Arundel House in the Strand in London. Apart from this town palace (its sprawling courtyards and gardens covered over three acres), the 12th Earl also had Henry VIII's palace of Nonsuch which was given to him by Queen Mary, in addition to Arundel Castle itself.

At Arundel the 12th and last of the Fitzalan earls was responsible for saving the Fitzalan Chapel from destruction. In December 1544, a year before the Act abolishing chantries, he successfully petitioned the king and bought back the chapel, college and all its endowments for 1,000 marks. It has been the private property of his successors ever since, though the remainder of the building is the parish church. At the castle he embarked on a thorough reconstruction of the old residential buildings to make a Tudor mansion. This may have been carried out in two phases, the first in the 1540s and the second in the 1570s. He built a fourth range in the south bailey to make a complete quadrangle. It stood at the foot of the motte and was of brick with mullion windows and tall polygonal chimney-stacks like Hampton Court. In the east range he made a long gallery on the first floor 121 ft. long and 12 ft. wide, reflecting the latest architectural fashion from France and Italy. All the family rooms in the south wing were remodelled, probably in the 1570s, when large mullion and transom windows were inserted to let in more light.

Very little of the 12th Earl's work has survived later alterations, for, whereas the Norman work was treated with a certain amount of reverence even in the destructive 18th century, the Tudor work was thought to be neither 'modern' nor 'venerable' so was swept away, partly by utilitarian considerations, and then by burgeoning antiquarian taste. A good impression of the exterior of the castle as remodelled in the mid-16th century can,

14 *Lady Mary Fitzalan who married the 4th Duke of Norfolk. After Hans Eworth.*

however, be gleaned from 18th-century topographical paintings and engravings made before the residential part of the castle was transformed out of all recognition by the 18th- and 19th-century Dukes of Norfolk.

Chapter II
The Howard Era

The 12th Fitzalan Earl was the last of his line, for his only son died aged 18 in Brussels on 13 June 1556. But the 12th Earl also had two daughters, Jane and Mary. Jane the elder married Lord Lumley, who like his father-in-law was a Catholic recusant with antiquarian tastes. The younger, Mary, married Thomas Howard, 4th Duke of Norfolk, but died of a puerperal fever in 1557 after the birth of a son Philip. The Lumleys did not have any children, so Philip was left as the eventual sole heir of his grandfather Henry, Earl of Arundel. In 1570 Lord Arundel made an agreement with his son-in-law, the Duke of Norfolk whereby Arundel and the estates, though with a life-interest to Lord Lumley, would be entailed on Philip and his heirs. This cost the duke £8,000 and the promise that the Earldom of Arundel would take precedence over the Earldom of Surrey (which had been re-created for the Howards at the same time as the Dukedom of Norfolk, by Richard III in 1483).

Two years after signing the agreement with Lord Arundel the Duke of Norfolk was executed for treason having become entangled in the Ridolfi Plot to replace Elizabeth on the throne with her Catholic cousin Mary Queen of Scots. His titles and all the Howard estates were attainted by the Crown. When his Fitzalan grandfather died in 1580, however, Philip succeeded to the Earldom of Arundel, and his Fitzalan inheritance was not affected by his father's attainder as it came to him through his mother. In 1580 Philip came to an amicable arrangement with Lord Lumley whereby his uncle gave up his life-interest in Arundel in return for an annuity. Philip thus found himself in complete ownership of the castle as well as Arundel House in London, and most of the Fitzalan Sussex estates. Lord Lumley on the other hand inherited outright Nonsuch Palace, Stansted near Chichester (which had been a hunting lodge of the medieval Earls of Arundel) and the 12th Earl's great library (which in due course was bought by James I for

Henry Frederick, the Prince of Wales, and now forms part of the British Library).

Philip, Earl of Arundel, also received back from the Crown some of his father's estates including the great house built by the 3rd Duke at Kenninghall in Norfolk which he used as his main seat and where he entertained Queen Elizabeth. He spent time at Arundel as well, however, and it was there that he re-embraced the Catholic faith. He had been baptised a Catholic, indeed King Philip II of Spain was his godfather, but he had been brought up and educated at Cambridge as a Protestant. Arundel Castle had advantages for a nobleman with Catholic leanings. It was close to the coast and so was accessible for priests from the continent and

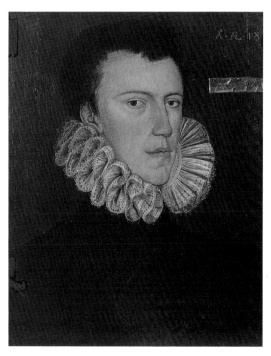

15 St Philip Howard, Earl of Arundel who inherited Arundel Castle from his Fitzalan grandfather.

also offered the opportunity for escape in a boat, if the occasion required it. Philip is supposed finally to have made up his mind on the religious question while pacing up and down his grandfather's long gallery in the east wing of the castle.

In Philip's time the castle remained much as it was in his grandfather's day, the rooms well-furnished with tapestries, oak, walnut and marquetry furniture. When Philip inherited in 1580 a detailed inventory was drawn up by Thomas Cowper, the Yeoman of the Garderobe at Arundel, and three commissioners sent down for the purpose from London. They listed the contents of the principal rooms anti-clockwise, beginning with the hall in the west wing and then moving on to the family apartments in the south wing, the long gallery and Percy Lodgings in the east wing, and ending with the bed chambers in the gatehouse and in the west range at the north end of the hall. It is worth quoting this inventory (now preserved in the British Library, MS Lansdowne, XXX No.83) at length, for it gives the clearest indication of the interior of the castle before partial destruction in the Civil War:

The inventorie indented taken this xxth day of the moneth of July, in the xxiid year of the reigne of our soveraigne lady, Elizabeth, queene, made between William Norton, Henry Russell, and Robert Whytney, Commissioners of Philippe, Erle of Arundell, on the one parte, and Thomas Cowper, servante to the said Erle, and yeoman of the Garderobe of the Castle of Arundell, on the other parte.

The Great Hall—Imprimis, Hangings of sundry ancient stories iii peeces. Item, vi tables upon standing tressels, wth benches next the wall. Item, one paier of great andyrons of yron. Item, hanging of olde stories vi peeces. Item, ii Turkie carpetts for the round windowe, and one olde one for the other window. Item, one great Turkie foote-carpett under the table, and one uppon the table there. Item, ii Turkie carpetts uppo~ the cubberd. Item, one faire long quishion for the windowe, wth my lord of Arundell his armes imbrodered wth golde and silver. Item, i long quishion of crymson wrought velvet, and one little quishion of the same. Item, one chaire and quishion blacke velvett, fringed with blacke and yellowe. Item, one chaire of blewe velvett. Item, ii long tables of firre uppo~ tressels. Item, xvi joined stooles of waynescotte. Item, ii joined formes of oke. Item, i paier of andyrons of brasse. Item, ii cubberds of oke.

The Olde Chappell—Item, iii peeces of hanginge of sundry olde stories. Item, i joined fourme of oke. Item, ii joined stooles of wainescotte.

The Tower Chambre—Item, v peeces of hanginge. Item, thre windowe-clothes of greene clothe. Item, i pallet-case of canvas, i fetherbedd and boulster thereto, i covering of parke-worke, i rugge for a blancket. Item, i cubberd of oke. Item, ii lowe stooles of crymson wrought velvett. Item, ii lowe stooles of clothe of bodkyne, wherof one of greene velvett of the same stuffe.

The Lord Lumleyes Chambre—Item, i peece of hanging of the vii planetts. Item, i olde windowe-clothe of parke-worke. Item, i bedd of crymson taffata, wth v curtyans, and valens thereto, and one counterpointe of the same stuffe, lined wth fustia~. Item, i fetherbedd and boulster, ii pillowes of tike, i pallet-case of canvas, ii white rugges for blanckets, and one woole bedd of white canvas. Item, i little quishio~ of wrought velvett. Item, i joined stoole. Item, i close-stoole and ii chamb~ pottes.

The Square Chambre—Item, iii peeces of hangings of okes and white horses. Item, i bedsteeds of wallnut-tree, wth tester of crymson velvett imbrodered wth cloth of golde, and v crymson silk curtians wth one counterpoynt of crymson taffata lined with white fustia~, to the same. One chier (chair) and two long cusshians of the same stuffe to the same bedd. Item, i fetherbedd and boulster, i pillowe, iii rugges, and ii fustia~ blancketts thereto. Item, i pallett bedd uppo~ the floore, i boulster, i covering of verders, and one pallet-case of canvas. Item, one olde cubberd of waynescotte. Item, one carpett of greene clothe for the cubberd. Item, i paier of andirons of iron. Item, i close-stoole, xiii chamb~ pottes.

The Daunsing Chambre—Item, v peeces of hanginge of imegerye. Item, i great Turkey ffoote-carpett. Item, i chier and long quishion of crimson wrought velvett, and three little quishions of the same stuffe. Item, iii long joined formes of oke, and v joined stooles. Item, ii long tables uppo~ tressells. Item, i square table uppo~ tressells, and a greene carpett thereto. Item, i paier of latin andyrons.

The King's Chambre—Item, hangings of oke leaves and Matravers knotts v peeces. Item, i bedd of oke and pallet-case, i fetherbed and boulster, i pillowe, i wolle bedd, and ii rugges for blancketts. Item, i sparner, wth double valence of redd and greene taffata, iii curtyans of greene silke, and i quilt thereto. Item, i cubberd of oke, and Turkeye carpett thereto. Item, i chaier of blacke lether. Item, i close-stoole and chamb~ pott.

The Cage Chambre—Item, hanginge of parke-worke v peeces. Item, i pallet-case of canvas, i fetherbed and boulster, i covering of verders lined wth canvas, i white rugge. Item, i cubberd of oke, and a greene carpett. Item, ii joined formes of oke.

The Gallerye—viii hangings of greene clothe, bordered wth sarcenett. Item, vi wallnut-tree chaiers, wth marke-tree [stoole?]. Item, i square table of marke-tree, wth a frame. Item, i cubberd of wallnut-tree. Item, vi joined stooles of wallnut-tree. Item, iii chaiers of blacke lether.

The Gallerye Chambre—Item, hangings of ffynes verders v peeces of smaller fflowers. Item, i bedsteede of wainescott, i sparner of clothe of bawdkyn and imbrodered wth starres, iii curtyans of murrey silke and one quilte of silke, one chaier and quishion of blewe...clothe, and i quishion of the same. Item, i Turkey carpett for the windowe. Item, i square quishio~ of clothe of goulde and silver for the windowe. Item, i cubberd of oke, and a Turkey carpett [insert above last two words - sent to London] for it. Item, i fetherbedd, i boulster, ii woolbedds, ii pillowes, i rugge, and ii fustia~ blancketts. Item, i Turkey foote-carpett at the bedds feete. Item, i joined stoole of wainescotte. Item, i fetherbedd, boulster, and i covering of imagerye [insert above last three words—lost by Thomas Cooper].

The Percyes Hall—Item, hangings of smale verders vi peeces of small fflowers. Item, i sparner of small verders wth double valence of fflowers, and iii curtyans of sarcenett, and one very large counterpoint of smale verders wth fflowers and wth armes. Item, i large quilt of olde silke to the same. Item, i fetherbedd and boulster very large. Item, ii windowe-clothes of greene clothe. Item, i paier of andirons of yron. Item, i joined stoole.

The Percyes Chambre—Item, hangings of auncient stories v peeces. Item, i sparner of clothe of bawdkyn wth curtyans of greene silke, and one covering of the same stuffe. Item, i lardge quilte of olde silke, and i counterpointe of greene carcenett. Item, i bedsteede of bordes, i pallet-case of canvas, ii ruggs for blancketts, i fetherbedd, and i boulster. Item, a windowe-clothe of greene clothe. Item, i cubberd of oke, and a greene clothe for the same. Item, i olde forme, and iii joined stooles.

The Percies Inner chambre—Item, hangins of parke-worke and imergerye iii peeces. Item, i bedsteede of bordes, i fetherbedd, i boulster, i rugg, and i covering. Item, i close-stoole, and a chamb~ potte.

Beaumonds Tower—Item, hangings of verders iii peeces. Item, i bedsteede of oke, i fetherbedd, i boulster and rugge for a blanckett, and one canopy and quilt to the same. Item, i peece of verders of clear leaves.

The Chambre in Beaumonds Tower above—Item, i bedd, i boulster, i rugge for a blanckett, and one canopy and covering of greene silke to the same. Item, i cubberd of oke, wth a little green clothe [insert above last two words - sent to London]. Item, hangings of greene clothe bordered with sarcenett iiii peeces.

The Receivors Chambre—Item, hangins of smale verders i peece, and i peece of imagerye. Item, ii bedds, ii boulsters, i tester of silke, paned redd white and blacke, wth one greene silke quilt, olde and i covering.

The Chambre next the Gate—Item, hangins of brode leaves v peeces. Item, i cubberd of oake, and i Turkey carpett [insert above last two words - sent to London]. Item, i greene clothe for the windowe. Item, i bedsteede of wainescotte, wth tester of redd tynsalle, and iii curtians of redd silke and one quilt of silke to the same, i quishio~ of tynsalle. Item, ii fetherbedds, ii boulster, ii rugges for blancketts, and i covering of verders.

The Upper Chambre ov~ the Gate—Item, hangings of imegerye v peeces. Item, i bedsteede of waynescott, i tester of blewe velvett and clothe of goulde, wth iii short curtians and a quilt of blewe silke, with one chaire and long cusshio~ suteable, i bedd, i boulster, and i rugge. Item, i bedd, i boulster, i ruge, and it covering of course imegerye. Item, i cubberd of oke, and i Turkey carpett [insert above last two words—sent to London].

The Chambre at the Hall-End—Item, hangings of the story of king David v peeces. Item, one other peece of the same storie. Item, i bedsteede of oke, i bedd and boulster, i Venice rugge, i olde quilte of silke tawnie, and i olde tester of redd and russett satten. Item, i cubberd of oke, wth a Turkey carpett.

The next Chambre to the Hall-End. item, hangings of parke-worke and verders v peeces. Item, i bedsteede of oake, i tester of yellowe satten, with i bedd and i boulster, i covering of olde imegerye. Item, i cubberd of oke, and a carpett of greene clothe thereto.

(Signed)   William Norton.
            Henry Russell
            Robert Whytney

Five years later Philip was arrested at sea, having left for the continent in a boat from Littlehampton, the port at the mouth of the River Arun. It was an offence to leave the country without the permission of the queen. He was fined £10,000 and imprisoned in the Tower. At the time of the Armada in 1588 he was tried for treason and condemned to death, his earldom and estates being attainted. Though the queen never signed the death warrant and the sentence was never carried out, he died of dysentery after ten years' imprisonment in the Tower in 1595. His only son, Thomas, was born after he was imprisoned, so he never saw him. Thomas was brought up by his widowed mother Anne Countess of Arundel in straitened circumstances, but on the accession to the throne of James I he was restored as Earl of Arundel, and the castle and Sussex estate were returned to him in 1604. He rarely visited the castle, however, and it was not much inhabited by the family between 1585 and the return of the Dukes of Norfolk to live there on a more permanent basis two hundred years later in the 1780s.

Thomas, known to posterity as 'the Collector Earl', kept the castle and Fitzalan Chapel in reasonable repair. The hall, for instance was restored in 1635. He made a new burial vault under the chapel to which (with royal permission) be brought his father's body from the Tower, and where the Howard family has continued to be buried down to the present. He also obtained an Act of Parliament in 1627 to entail the Earldom, Honour, Castle and lands of Arundel in the Howard family in perpetuity. That part of the Act referring to the castle and land was repealed in 1959 (in order to avoid death duties) but the descent of the Earldom and the Honour continues to devolve according to the 1627 Act. Lord Arundel also settled a sum of £100 a year for the repair of the castle and the Fitzalan Chapel.

In 1642 at the beginning of the Civil War the Collector Earl accompanied Princess Mary, daughter of Charles I, to her husband William of Orange in the Low Countries. He never returned to England, but journeyed on to Padua where he spent his remaining days. A year after his departure, in December 1643, the castle was twice besieged, first by a Royalist force under Hopton who took possession, then by a Parliamentarian force under the command of General Waller. The Royalist garrison held out for 17 days before surrendering, in the course of which some damage was done to the buildings, but the residential ranges were repaired for the occupation of a Parliamentary garrison, and for storing gunpowder, till 1653 when the troops were withdrawn and most of the powder removed to Portsmouth. Some of it was used to blow up the western part of the defences. The Council of State had ordered on 7 October that 'the walls and workes of Arundell Castle should forthwith be slighted'. On 17 November it ordered 'the keys of the house of Arundell Castle to be delivered unto Mr Howard the fortifycations of the said castle being demolished'. This was Henry Howard, later 6th Duke of Norfolk, grandson of the Collector Earl who had died in Padua in 1646. The 'Collector's' body had been brought back and buried in the Fitzalan Chapel. His 'interiores', removed in order to embalm the body, were interred in St Anthony's basilica in Padua where they are commemorated by an inscribed stone in the cloisters. The Collector, in his will, had asked for an elaborate tomb with a bronze statue by Fanelli to be erected to his memory in the Fitzalan

16 The Collector Earl and his classical statues, 1617, *by Daniel Mytens.*

Chapel but, because of the unsettled times in the aftermath of the Civil War, this was never executed.

The Howards were reinstated as Dukes of Norfolk by King Charles II at the Restoration in 1660. They did not live in the castle. The 5th Duke, whose mind was affected by a fever contracted while studying at Padua, never returned to England but lived in Italy for the rest of his life. The 6th and 7th Dukes had houses in Norwich, Surrey and London where they spent their time. Though occasional repairs were done to some of the buildings, materials were also taken away for use elsewhere, including lead and timber from the roof to Henry Howard's villa at Albury near Guildford in the 1660s. Many of the buildings remained in ruins.

In the early 18th century Thomas, 8th Duke of Norfolk considered plans for completely rebuilding the castle as a grand new house, to the design of James Gibbs. This was not proceeded with, and instead the duke patched up part of the ruins as an occasional residence where he could stay from time to time when overseeing estate business. He and his brother and successor, Edward the 9th Duke, did not spend more than two weeks a year at Arundel. The exact date of his repairs is not known but they must have taken place *c.*1718. He added a new red brick front to the courtyard side of the south wing, with regular sash windows and two rusticated entrances to the staff quarters on the ground floor. The main purpose of this addition was to improve the circulation of the family rooms by making a broad access gallery on the first floor. The old chapel was brought back into use, for the duke was a Catholic, to serve not just the family and household but the local Catholic population as well. The chapel was well fitted up. The painted altarpiece of the Nativity was by Gennari and came from James II's Catholic chapel at Whitehall. The set of altar plate was made by the London silversmith Charles Kandler. Kandler also made the gilt baroque tabernacle to the design of James Gibbs in 1730. Successive 18th-century dukes maintained a priest at Arundel, who had his own apartment, next to the chapel and the Library, at the west end of the new gallery. The rooms within the shell of Henry II's building were repaired to serve as a drawing room and dining room. The old long gallery in the east wing became the entrance hall with a pedimented front door in the central bay window, approached by a flight of steps from the quadrangle. The west range was left as a shell but various lean-tos erected inside served as stables and a coach-house.

The 8th Duke also carried out some improvements in the grounds. He demolished the 16th-century brick range on the north side of the quadrangle, which was no doubt in poor condition by that date, in order to open up the view of the motte and keep. The quadrangle itself was grassed over and a sun dial erected in the middle. The north bailey on the other side of the keep was laid out within the old walls as a formal kitchen garden and at the north end several stepped terraces were created, which still exist and from which it was possible to admire the view over the curtain walls to the river valley in one direction, and the sea in the other. Outside the castle, the Little Park was replanted and a series of walks with trees and shrubs was formed along the Norman earthworks and the steep bank between the castle and the ancient mill pond at Swanbourne on the east side of the castle.

In the 18th century Arundel was very much a subsidiary house of the family. The principal seat of the Norfolks was Worksop Manor, in the Dukeries in Nottinghamshire, which had been brought to the Howards as part of the inheritance of Aletheia Talbot, wife of the 'Collector' Earl, who was the daughter and eventually the sole heiress of Gilbert, 7th Earl of Shrewsbury. Her inheritance included large estates in Derbyshire, Yorkshire and Nottinghamshire, including Sheffield and Worksop Manor which was a spectacular Elizabethan 'prodigy house' built for her grandfather, the 6th Earl of Shrewsbury, by Robert Smythson. The 8th Duke remodelled and embellished Worksop to create a baroque palace with painted decorations by Jacques Parmentier and rich new furniture (some of which is now at Arundel), as well as grand formal gardens with avenues, statues, and ironwork by Tijou. He also bought the house in St James's Square which was to be the town residence of the Dukes of Norfolk until its sale over 200 years later in 1938. Eighteenth-century Arundel was a second or third fiddle to these grander and more fashionable houses. It was treated by the 8th and 9th Dukes as a cross

17   The 8th Duke of Norfolk *by Van Bleeck.*

between a museum and jumble store. Rather in the way that the Dukes of Devonshire used Elizabethan Hardwick as a receptacle for unfashionable furniture displaced from Chatsworth, or the Earls of Mount Edgcumbe used medieval Cotehele for out-of-date chattels from Mount Edgcumbe, so the Dukes of Norfolk sent to Arundel old-fashioned sets of chairs or worn out tapestries, which were too good to throw away, yet not smart enough for use at London or Worksop. In this way there was a deliberate effort to maintain its ancient and antiquarian atmosphere. The Howards also continued to be buried in the Fitzalan Chapel, the bodies of the 8th and 9th Dukes and their wives and relations all being brought down after death from London or wherever and interred in the vault there. As Catholics, their funerals had to be low-key and no monuments were erected to them, nor was the chapel itself kept in more than weatherproof condition, for fear of drawing too much attention to its papist associations.

Though the family seems to have appreciated some of the picturesque quality and antique atmosphere of the castle and its surroundings, not everybody else did. Horace Walpole who might have been expected to enthuse about the castle was disappointed by it, nor did he care much for Sussex either. After a visit to the castle he wrote: 'It is now only a heap of ruins, with a new indifferent apartment clapt up for the Norfolks, when they reside there for a week or a fortnight ... Sussex is a great damper of curiosity'.

The 8th Duke of Norfolk died in 1732 and was succeeded by his younger brother Edward ('Ned') who had married Mary Blount (the daughter of Edward Blount of Blagdon in Devon). The duke was shy and bookish and occupied himself by doing all his own estate business directly. The duchess, by contrast, was a strong, extrovert character. Horace Walpole referred to her disrespectfully as 'My Lord Duchess', and Lord Rockingham quipped about a party at Norfolk House, 'Oh, there was all the company afraid of the duchess, and the Duke afraid of all the company'. Both were interested in the arts and architecture. To them is due much of the present contents of Arundel Castle including the books in the Library, the best 18th-century furniture and many of the paintings and portraits. They re-assembled the family collections after the vicissitudes of the previous century. Many of their things were at Worksop or

Norfolk House in their time and have only come to Arundel later; in the case of the contents of Worksop in 1838 and Norfolk House in 1938.

Their major project was the rebuilding of Norfolk House in St James's Square, London. They bought the adjoining Belasyse House to enlarge the site on which they constructed a large new house. Their architect was Matthew Brettingham, an English Palladian, who had constructed Holkham Hall for the Earl of Leicester in Norfolk. The plan of Norfolk House was an enlargement of the plan of the family and strangers' wings at Holkham with a circuit of living rooms and entertaining rooms opening conveniently off a central top-lit staircase hall. Brettingham's façade was an understated design of white brick with a top balustrade and pedimented windows. The interior by contrast was splendid. It was one of the finest rococo ensembles in London.

18 The 9th Duchess of Norfolk *by Vanderbank.*

19 *Norfolk House, London (destroyed).*

The shell of the house was finished in 1751 but the fitting up of the interior took a further five years. Brettingham was superseded as architect for this by an Italian, Gian Battista Borra, who came from Turin and worked in England largely for the circle of Frederick Prince of Wales. (The Prince and his wife were close friends of the Norfolks. His eldest son, the future King George III, was born in the old Norfolk House in May 1738 when the Wales's had been expelled from St James's Palace after a quarrel with George II.) Apart from Norfolk House, Borra was also responsible for several designs at Stowe in Buckinghamshire for Lord Temple who was also close to the Prince of Wales. Borra designed the wall decorations, chimneypieces, doorcases and the more architectural furniture at Norfolk House such as pier tables and looking-glass frames. The duchess herself was a strong force in the design of the rooms and was responsible for all the colour schemes and furnishings.

The house was rationally planned with rooms for everyday living on the ground floor and for grand entertaining on the first floor. The entrance hall was simply treated with a Doric frieze embellished with the Howard lion, Fitzalan horse and Talbot talbot hound in the metopes, copied from the background of a painting by Philip Fruytiers of

the Collector Earl and his family in the duke's collection. In the 18th century this frieze design was thought to be by Inigo Jones. (The frieze was saved when Norfolk House was demolished and is now in crates in the cellar at Arundel.)

The hall was austerely furnished with a set of mahogany hall chairs now in the Stone Hall at Arundel. To the left of the hall was the Dining Room with a simple rococo plaster ceiling and painted walls. Its chief feature was a set of ormolu pier tables and side-board elaborately decorated with grapes, goats' heads and other Bacchic symbols, which together with the matching pier glasses from between the windows are now in the Drawing Room at Arundel. To the right of the hall were two drawing rooms for everyday use. In contrast to the principal rooms upstairs where the furniture was all gilded, the seat furniture downstairs was of mahogany or walnut made by Joseph Metcalfe who supplied all the upholstered furniture at Norfolk House. Several of these sets of chairs are now at Arundel including a fine set with needlework after Aesop's fables in the Dining Room and, with contemporary Soho tapestry, in the Drawing Room. These rooms were hung with family portraits and three *capriccii* by Canaletto, all now at Arundel. The ground floor circuit was completed

20 *The Music Room from Norfolk House now in the Victoria
and Albert Museum.*

by the duke's own bedroom and dressing-room at the back facing the garden. These two were furnished with mahogany and were simpler than the rooms upstairs on the *piano nobile*.

The central staircase had large plaster cartouches on the walls designed by Borra and almost identical to some at the royal palace of the King of Sardinia at Stupinigi near Turin. The state rooms on the first floor formed a complete inter-connecting sequence right round the house, so that they could all be opened for a large reception, or just one or two used for cards and supper, if it was a smaller party. An ante-room led from the landing to the Music Room over the Dining Room. This was lined with white and gold rococo panelling designed by Borra and carved by Jean Antoine Cuenot, from Piedmont, who came to England with Borra and was responsible for all the carving at Norfolk House including the frame furniture, pier glasses and the picture frames which now grace many of the family portraits at Arundel. The Music Room was saved when the house was demolished in 1938 and is now in the Victoria and Albert Museum where Cuenot's carvings and Thomas Clarke's ceiling plasterwork can still be admired.

Beyond the Music Room and filling the rest of the frontage to the square was a pair of drawing rooms treated *en suite*. Both had gilded plaster ceilings designed by Brettingham and chimney-pieces and looking-glasses designed by Borra. The first room was hung with green damask and the second with crimson cut velvet, with the curtains and upholstery to match. The idea of treating rooms with different co-ordinated colour schemes was an idea of the duchess and was considered to be very novel at the time. Borra designed similar sets of pier tables to go between the windows in both rooms, one pair with inlaid grey marble tops and the other with white marble tops. These are now in the East Drawing Room and east passage at Arundel. The large set of gilt seat furniture in the French manner distributed between the two rooms was based on engravings by Boffrand. Much of it has been dispersed, but one of the large sofas is in the Victoria Room at Arundel and some of the smaller chairs in the dower house at Arundel Park. The large French looking-glasses, 'the largest plates ... that were ever brought over' costing £1,000 a set, were sold in 1938 as was the out-of-fashion collection of *seicento* paintings which hung here. Whereas the family rooms downstairs had English

21 *Chinese looking-glass from the State Bedroom at Norfolk House.*

portraits and 'modern' topographical paintings, 18th-century fashionable taste dictated that the state rooms should display the works of Italian and Flemish masters. The Collector Earl's incomparable paintings had all been dispersed in the previous century, in the aftermath of the Civil War and various family squabbles. The 9th Duke filled the gap by forming a new collection *en bloc* through an agent in Italy. They were sent by sea from Leghorn (Livorno) in 1750. (The customs bill is preserved in the archives at Arundel.) Of variable quality they looked good *in toto*, and were hung in the decorative 18th-century manner in three tiers with the largest in the middle, smaller canvases below, and those with circular or oval frames arranged symmetrically.

Behind the cut velvet Drawing Room was the Great Room or saloon which was used for dancing and similar entertainments. It was hung with four panels of Gobelins tapestry of the *Nouvelle Indes* series, which the duchess bought directly from the factory for £9 a yard. She went frequently to Paris, for she was very francophile and was received at Versailles by Louis XV. The doorcases (designed by Borra and carved by Cuenot) echoed the animals in the tapestry as they were carved with monkeys

22 Capriccio from the Family Drawing Room at Norfolk House *by Canaletto.*

holding garlands of grapes and pomegranates. One of these is now in the Victoria and Albert Museum, and the tapestries are at Arundel (divided between the Grand Staircase and the Barons' Hall). The two magnificent gilt pier tables from the Great Room with carved and gilt frames and delicious-looking, almost edible, tops of Sicilian jasper are now in the Gallery at Arundel.

The sequence of state rooms at Norfolk House was completed by the bedroom and dressing room of the duchess, above the duke's and likewise facing the garden at the back. These were decorated in the Chinese taste with 'India papers' imported through the East India Company on the walls and painted satin hangings. A very fine Chinese looking-glass from here is now in the York Bedroom at Arundel. The commode in the 'French taste' from the duchess's bedroom is probably that now in the Upper Gallery at Arundel.

The Norfolks gave a great house-warming at Norfolk House in 1756 to celebrate its completion. Horace Walpole, who was so unen-

thusiastic about Arundel, was among the guests and was ecstatic: 'All the earth was there. You would have thought there had been a comet, everybody was gazing in the air and treading on one another's toes. In short, you never saw such a scene of magnificence and taste. The tapestry, the embroidered bed, the illumination, the glasses, the lightness and novelty of the ornaments, and the ceilings are delightful'.

The Norfolks did not stop building work in 1756. A few years later they called in the architect James Paine who, though not himself a Catholic, worked for many Catholic patrons including Lord Petre at Thornden in Essex and Lord Arundell at Wardour in Wiltshire. In 1764 Paine designed a large new Catholic chapel at the back of Norfolk House and also designed a thorough remodelling of the interior of Worksop which was completed by summer 1761 when the duke and duchess gave a party attended by the Duke of York. Shortly afterwards a fire broke out there and Worksop was burnt to the ground. Undaunted, the duke and

23   Worksop Manor, 1777 *by William Hodges.*

duchess embarked on a vast scheme to rebuild it as a quadrangular palace to Paine's design. If completed, it would have been the largest house in England since Blenheim. But after one wing was habitable work was stopped because of the death of the Norfolks' nephew and immediate heir, Edward Howard. (They had no children of their own.) The interior of the new Worksop was furnished in the height of fashion, again under the direction of the duchess, and, as at Norfolk House, she gave every room its own co-ordinated colour scheme.

Some of the old contents of Worksop were destroyed in the 1761 fire, but others were rescued, and new things bought. The 9th Duke formed a completely new library between 1762 and 1777 to replace his old books lost in the flames, as the fire had broken out in the room next to the library in the old house. The furnishing of the new house at Worksop led to a general re-arrangement of furniture and pictures between the three family houses. Some things were brought to Worksop from Norfolk House, while various old-fashioned items, including the 8th Duke's grand early 18th-century

sets of gilt gesso and needlework chairs were sent to Arundel (where they still are, in the Barons' Hall and Gallery respectively). A feature of Worksop, which reflected the duchess's interest in the East India Company and investment in trading expeditions, was that every bed and dressing room had a Chinese or Japanese lacquered cabinet or coffer (many of which are now at Arundel).

The 9th Duke and Duchess also used James Paine to design some improvements at Arundel in the 1760s, the chief of which was the embellishment of the chapel which was given a coved plaster ceiling and an architectural altarpiece with gilded Ionic columns supporting a pediment, as a frame for the Gennari Nativity. Paine also designed some new decorations for the Drawing Room, breakfast room and one or two others in the south wing, including painted overdoors in *trompe l'oeil* by Theodore de Bruyn, a Flemish artist brought to England by the duchess, who also decorated the staircase hall at the new Worksop. The other rooms retained their previous character, which was enhanced by old-fashioned tapestries

24   *The exterior of Arundel Castle c.1770 by James Canter.*

and hangings as well as the duchess's own needlework. It may have been at this time that the few surviving Fitzalan heirlooms were concentrated at Arundel, including 16th-century portraits of Henry 12th Earl of Arundel and his son Lord Maltravers who predeceased him, and the 14th-century sword, nicknamed 'Mongley', which still hangs in the Armoury today.

Under the terms of the will of the 9th Duke who died in 1777, detailed inventories of the contents of Worksop, Norfolk House and Arundel Castle were made to form the basis of their being entailed as chattels to descend with the dukedom. It is possible therefore to glean a very clear picture of where all the things were in his lifetime, many of which have since come to Arundel from the other houses. On his death he was succeeded by a cousin, Charles Howard of Greystoke in Cumberland, who became 10th Duke of Norfolk and who was to initiate the revival of Arundel Castle as the principal family seat after 200 years of comparative neglect. Four years after the 9th Duke's death, in 1781 Mr Lahy, the estate steward, wrote a letter to the *Lewes Journal* refuting the Arundel parish officer's rating description of the castle as a 'princely palace'. He pointed out that the officer could not 'persuade those who have the happiness to be endowed with sight, that a mouldering pile of ruins is a princely palace; suppose, I say, this venerable pile of ruins,

for such everyone must allow it to be, which the Dukes of Norfolk only visit *en passant*'. It was not to remain in this state for much longer; but in 1785, before it was altered, the 25-year-old Elizabeth Collett, who was doing a tour of picturesque spots in a post-chaise, visited the castle and left an amusing description of what she saw.

We then proceeded for Arundel, where we saw the Castle, the seat of the Duke of Norfolk, a part of which & the tower on which are Battlements very ancient, supposed to have been built by the Saxons in the year 800. In the middle of the Tower is a large cavity underground called the giant's cave, but we did not choose to go down it; there is also a deep well which has a most horrible appearance when you look into it. The furniture of the house is by no means modern; a great deal of good needlework in chairs, sofas, etc., the colours in high preservation, & the most knotting in fringes I ever saw anywhere, in the work of the late Duchess. We were much surprised in viewing the Chapel to find a lamp burning, which told us the family were Roman Catholicks, tho' the Duke had read his recantation in order to take his seat in the House of Peers [she was muddling the pious Duke with his scapegrace son Charles, who had indeed 'conformed' to become M.P. for Carlisle]; there are several of that persuasion in the town who worship with them. The House is pleasantly situated, the prospects round extensive; there is a glass chandelier kept for the curiosity of it being the first that was ever made; it begins to look very shabby & wants dusting very much.

Chapter III
Revival

The 10th Duke did not like Worksop and rarely went there. He already had his own estates at Greystoke Castle in Cumberland and the Deepdene in Surrey where he continued to spend most of his time. At the Deepdene he built a comfortable suburban villa to the design of William Gowan, a London surveyor of no great distinction. He liked Arundel, however. He had antiquarian and literary tastes which the 'venerable ruins' were guaranteed to inspire. He stayed at the castle in June 1779 and spent Christmas there in 1781, when the household bills came to over £500. He determined to restore the castle as a proper country house. In 1783 he secured by Act of Parliament a sum of up to £5,000 from the renewal of the leases of the Arundel House estate in the Strand (which had been developed as four streets of houses by the 6th Duke in the late 17th century) for the purpose of repairing Arundel. But his death in 1786 prevented anything substantial being done, and it was left to his son Charles who succeeded as 11th Duke of Norfolk (known to posterity as 'the Drunken Duke') to restore Arundel Castle as the principal ducal seat. He embarked on the project as soon as he inherited in 1787 and it remained his hobby for the rest of his life, doing only as much work each year as he had allocated money for: £1,282 in 1802, £1,218 in 1803, £1,304 in 1804 and so on till his death in 1815.

25   View of the Castle from Swanbourne Lake *by William Daniell.*

26   The Quadrangle in 1824 *by William Daniell.*

He created the present park as well as rebuilding the residential part of the castle. His restoration of Arundel parallels George III's work at Windsor and that of several other landowners who turned to castle-building near the end of the 18th century. They were mainly Tories, and were attracted to the castle style because of its traditional and feudal associations. The Duke of Norfolk, however, was drawn to the Gothic and castles for the opposite reasons. To him they represented ancient liberties, trial by jury, and the moderating influence of the barons on the royal prerogative. The subjects chosen for sculpture and stained glass at Arundel left no doubt of the duke's intentions. A Coade stone statue of Liberty, 12 ft. high, greeted the visitor from a niche over the front door. The east wing was dominated by a Coade stone relief modelled by J.C.F. Rossi showing *King Alfred Instituting Trial by Jury on Salisbury Plain*, while the west wing comprised the Barons' Hall, with stained glass windows commemorating the signing of Magna Carta. Its foundation stone was dedicated in Latin 'to Liberty asserted by the Barons in the reign of John'.

The restoration work was done in stages: first the park in 1787, then the south front in 1791, the north front in 1795, the east wing containing the Library in 1801, the west wing with the Barons' Hall in 1806 and the new gatehouse in 1809. The last was never finished, and the castle was left incomplete at the duke's death. The painter and diarist, William Farington, who visited in 1811 wrote: 'Arundel Castle is in a very imperfect state, not to say comfortless. There are a few rooms only fit to be occupied'. At Arundel a team of skilled craftsmen from the duke's estate in Cumberland was assembled to carry out his plans. The Earl Marshal's secretary, James Dallaway, a historian who helped in tracking down suitable historical models to copy, wrote: 'the Duke had resolved to form the whole upon his own design, and he accordingly selected from his own estates at Greystoke in Cumberland [craftsmen] whom he placed under architects and sculptors in London until they were perfect in their art—viz. Mr J. Teasdale architect, his brother a sculptor of ornament in marble, and J. Ritson and his son in mahogany'.

The duke also consulted various other experts on his proposals. In 1787, he entertained Richard Gough, the Oxford antiquary, and the Gothic architect, Francis Hiorne, at Greystoke, 'relative to his intended repairs at Arundel Castle'. They visited various buildings in the north, including Alnwick Castle, which Paine and Adam had restored for the Duke of Northumberland. Hiorne made plans for Arundel that involved demolishing all the south quadrangle, retaining only the 12th-century keep on its motte, and building a new Gothic house in the north bailey. Fortunately nothing came of this destructive proposal, and Hiorne's work at Arundel was restricted to a triangular prospect tower, which still bears his name, built in the new park in 1787 and recently restored.

Horace Walpole, too, gave the duke advice and recommended James Wyatt. The duke, however, had no very high opinion of Wyatt, and was responsible with John Carter and Sir Henry Englefield for blackballing him from the Society of Antiquaries, which George III referred to jokingly as a Popish Plot. In the event, 'after having long resolved in his own mind the idea of such a building, and resolved its various plans, he entrusted them for execution, solely to his ingenious master mason, and consulted none of the modern architects who have undertaken to revive the style and commanding effect of ancient English castles'.

Before starting work on the castle itself, the duke made the park and planted the surroundings, creating the magnificent setting which still largely exists. The old park, sometimes known as the Rewell Wood, lay to the west of the town, completely detached from the castle. It was converted into the home farm and provided with new buildings, the farmhouse being adorned with a Gothic bay window ascribed by the Royal Commission on Historic Monuments to the 16th century. In place of the Rewell Wood, the duke bought 1,145 acres of rabbit warren and rough grazing adjoining the castle to the north. He enclosed this area and created the present park from scratch.

This ambitious project involved a three-mile diversion of the London road as well as considerable planting of forest trees, new drives, lodges and a boundary wall. Belts of beech and yew cleverly emphasised the contours and framed the views through the downs to the sea, while the mill pond at Swanbourne was enlarged to form a lake.

27 The 11th Duke of Norfolk *by Gainsborough.*

28 *Hiorne's Tower in the Park, 1787.*

29 *Aerial view showing the park created by the 11th Duke.*

Dallaway described the results as 'presenting scenes worthy of Claude Lorraine or G. Smith'.

Work on the castle proper started in 1791 with the addition of the square south-east tower, which survived the Victorian remodelling though refenestrated, and the replanning of the south range to form an axial sequence of apartments: breakfast room, small and large drawing rooms, small and large dining rooms. The last was converted out of the former private chapel. (The 11th Duke conformed to the Established Church in order to sit in Parliament.) Though he removed the Catholic chapels from his houses, he provided alternative space in the outbuildings at Arundel in part of the old College buildings, and continued to pay the priests' wages. Behind these rooms the gallery was given a new bracketed ceiling of carved mahogany. Creevey who visited Arundel from Goodwood in 1828 thought the gallery the worst feature of 'that horrid, benighted castle ... 190 feet long of the most dingy oak and a window at the top of each end to light it, And everything else in the place equally dismal'. Though since remodelled, the Georgian disposition of the state rooms at Arundel determines their present plan. The architectural style of the new parts of the castle, like the

iconography of the decorative features, was determined by the 11th Duke's Whig principles. It was a hybrid of Perpendicular Gothic and Norman (then called 'Saxon'), both of which were associated in the duke's eyes with ancient liberty.

The two styles were combined in a naïve attempt to suggest chronological development, with 'Saxon' being used at ground-floor level and Perpendicular for the *piano nobile*. The three new courtyard façades, arranged like the backdrops to a stage setting, were all richly carved by the John Teasdales, father and son, with lively corbels, label stops and rich dogtooth moulding to the arches, while the parapet was pierced with the cross crosslets fitchy of the Howard arms. After the completion of the work at Arundel, John Teasdale junior moved to London to work on the restoration of Henry VII's Chapel at Westminster.

A special feature of the 11th Duke's work, and one redolent of his interests as president of the Society of Arts, was the large programme of stained glass windows, the most ambitious undertaken in a private house at that date, though not all of it was completed; Francis Eginton's intended windows depicting the nine muses, for instance, were never installed in the Library. Eginton's glass in the great south window of the Dining Room was erected, but it only survived for 40 years before it was removed to spare Queen Victoria's blushes. It was designed by William Hamilton, and showed the entertainment of a buxom Queen of Sheba by King Solomon, in which the central figure was a portrait of the duke himself, complete with bushy side-whiskers. This was why Horace Walpole nicknamed the duke 'Solomon'.

The stained glass in the Barons' Hall was designed by J. Lonsdale and made by Joseph Backler. The small side windows depicted 'the Barons' (all portraits of the Howard family), while the 'Great Norfolk Window' at the north end showed King John, 'with an expression of strong revulsion', being forced to sign Magna Carta by further portraits of the duke and his relations. The painter, John Constable, who visited the castle in 1834, thought

30 *(left)   The 11th Duke's front door, with Coade statues of Liberty and Hospitality (destroyed).*

31 *(below)   The Coade stone relief of Trial by Jury (destroyed).*

32   *Sebastopol Lobby and detail of stone carving by John Teasdale.*

Arundel Castle, our readers are probably aware was for many years the scene of the late Duke of Norfolk's trials at building; by which, as his own architect, he sought to instruct himself in the Gothic style. After being occupied in this way for upwards of forty years, and spending several hundred thousand pounds, he just arrived at last at that point where a man discovers his own utter ignorance ... Had the Duke employed an Architect, he would, no doubt have possessed a castle in a very superior taste, both externally and internally, to what Arundel Castle now is; but it does not follow, on that account, that he would have been so happy in seeing the more perfect works of his Architect, as he was in realising the crude ideas of his own mind'.

The Barons' Hall, like much of the 11th Duke's work, was demolished and replaced later in the 19th century, but his finest interior at Arundel, the noble Library 112 ft. long, was rightly admired and survives largely as designed by him. It is fitted out entirely in carved mahogany with a vault, aisles and transepts like the inside of an inflated wooden model for a Gothic church, and was inspired by St George's Chapel at Windsor. It occupies part of the shell of the Tudor long gallery. All the carving, including the naturalistic capitals and an appropriate display of strawberry leaves, was the work of the Jonathan Ritsons, senior and junior. Jonathan Ritson (junior), when the work at Arundel was completed, transferred to Petworth where he restored the Grinling Gibbons carvings for Lord Egremont who commissioned a portrait of him which still hangs in the Carved Room there.

The Duke of Norfolk's restoration campaign was described in an interesting article in the *St James's Chronicle*, published in August 1800, which unlike most of the descriptions of the 11th Duke's work at Arundel was actually complimentary, and saw his work as an attempt to preserve and restore the ancient character of the buildings:

Arundel Castle which is said to confer on its owner by the mere fact of its possession, the Earldom of Arundel, is now receiving such repairs and embellishments, as must render it the chief of ancient residences in England.

Perhaps no other building of equal date, has been retained in a habitable condition for so long a time, without having its appearance, in some degree perverted by additions and alterations inconsistent with the taste of the age in which it was built. Arundel Castle, on the contrary, is but maintained and continued by its present exterior improvements. Vast as they are, the design of the original founder is still obeyed, the new walls have risen upon the ancient model, and correspond with

these windows terrible and wrote to a friend: 'The Barons' Hall is a grand room, though strangely vulgarised by some hideous figures larger than life on painted glass; these ruffian-looking fellows look like drunken bargemen dressed up as Crusaders and are meant to represent the "Barons bold"'. John Claudius Loudon, writing in 1839, was even more damning about the whole of the 11th Duke's endeavours:

33   Picture Gallery before reconstruction.

the old ones in solidity of fabrick, as well as dignity of ornament. The successor of the Montgomery's, the Albeneys [sic] and the Fitz-Alans, has respected their taste, and that of the ages in which they here held dominion over their ample territories.

An entire new front of Massy stone differs from the others only in exhibiting the Insignia of the Howards, mixed with those of their predecessors. In raising this front, the Duke has taken an opportunity to enlarge the house and appears to have gained the space, now occupied on the basement storey, by a long range of servants' offices, including a new Kitchen, with two fire places and grates twelve or fourteen feet long. A new dining room, or rather hall, on the principal floor is also in this part of the building. The floor of this apartment is not yet fully laid, nor the walls stuccoed but a skirting of mahogany has been run along them, to the height of about 4 feet, and a musick gallery at the bottom is complete. This is one of the most sumptuous and appropriate of the interior improvements. It is constructed almost entirely of mahogany, richly carved

with the oak and the vine, and is supported by solid pillars of the same valuable material embraced by similar ornaments. A beautiful marble chimney-piece also displays some fine Bacchanalian imagery, but this was intended to be removed, being of a shape somewhat too modern for the style of the apartment, the stucco of which will be a dark brown—The Prince it is said, will be present at the first dinner that "warms" this room.

But of all the modes of liberal, and dignified expense, displayed in this mansion, that which is peculiar and distinguishing, is the use of the richest mahogany in almost every decoration, and for purposes to which ordinary wood is thought sufficient for the finest houses. Thus, the walls being more than six feet thick form a kind of frame to each window, which is five feet deep on the inside, and the whole of this spacious case—not excepting the top—is lined with mahogany over an inch in thickness. The window frames, which hold the magnificent plate glass panes, three feet in height each, are of course, of the same material and the solid mahogany doors are held in cases, which the thickness

34 *(above)   The Library designed by the 11th Duke.*

35 *(left)   Detail of mahogany carving by Jonathan Ritson.*

The Duke never finished his pet project. The Alfred Saloon beyond the Library was left a roofless shell; the gatehouse half its intended height; while his Barons' Hall and little chapel in the west wing were never fitted up internally. This did not prevent the duke from organising a great house-warming party in 1815, ostensibly to celebrate the 600th anniversary of Magna Carta. Like many of the duke's doings, this was an object of interest to the press, and the preparations were described in the *Courier* on 13 June 1815, which also gives a further description of the castle at that date:

Fete at Arundel Castle. Arundel, June 11 1815.—This afternoon at half-past six, his Grace the Duke of Norfolk arrived in his travelling-carriage, at the Castle. His Grace immediately on his arrival, inspected the preparations carrying on for the grand Fete, which will take place on Thursday next, the Anniversary of the day on which *King John*, and the Barons, signed Magna Carta. His Grace has caused to be erected a new room in the

of the inner walls renders, perhaps, four feet deep, all lined with panels of beautiful grain. It was once intended to floor all the best rooms with the most costly wood, but when it was tried in one apartment, the effect was found too gloomy. We shall not venture to estimate the value of this article disposed of in mere decoration. The Duke purchased it himself in the gross some years since.

Castle, called *The Barons' Room*, which is of great extent, though now in an unfinished state, and only capable of being fitted up in a temporary manner on the present occasion. It is, however, lined with scarlet, and the floor matted so as to form a magnificent, as well as a comfortable dinner-room; and in it the grand banquet will be served. On the window at the extremity of the room, fronting the Court-yard, is a superb painting, representing *King John* sitting, attended by the *Pope's Nuncio*, and the Barons while the King's Page, *Sir Hugh Montgomery*, presents the Duke of Norfolk of that date to the King. The likeness represented is a strong one of the present Duke.

The drawing-room, which will be appropriate for dancing, is a superb apartment, lined with crimson velvet, in panels framed with gold, in which is framed a series of family portraits. Chandeliers and glasses complete its magnificence. This room is also very extensive.

The Prince's room is lined with purple in gold panels.

The Library, which extends the whole length of the eastern side of the quadrangle, is of the present Duke's forming, his Grace's ancestors having left him few books. The receptacles for the books are also of his Grace's taste, and have been very lately finished. They are of the finest mahogany, modelled as it were, after the interior of Westminster Abbey, with Gothic fret-work and other carving of the highest and most exquisite workmanship.

The Duke has greatly extended the Castle on one side, which contains apartments for very numerous visitors. The front of this new erection is all of Bath and Portland stone, executed in a style perfectly corresponding with the remainder of the structure. Over the grand portal of the Castle are the figures of *Liberty* and *Hospitality*; by the first of which a Lyon reposes, and by the latter a *Horse*;–the two supporters of the arms of the Howards. The whole of this magnificent embellishment is in marble. Opposite to the entrance, and underneath a room appropriated to the Sciences, to Drawing, and to the other Arts, is a grand sculptural piece, representing *King Alfred*, dictating to his Chief Judge the Right of Jury. The Monarch is represented standing with the document in his left hand, written in Anglo-Saxon, and pointing with the forefinger of his right hand to the words which signify *Twelve Jurymen*. The Chief Judge, accompanied by the others, receives his Majesty's instructions, kneeling. The Twelve Jurymen form a group on one side of the composition. The whole is admirably executed, and has a majestic effect.

As it happens the Magna Carta dinner was the duke's swan song, and a few months later he died at Norfolk House, leaving his castle unfinished. He intended the Magna Carta dinner to reflect his

36   *The Staircase before Victorian reconstruction.*

Gothic Revival architecture and to 'renew and exhibit "the pomp of olden days"'. The new Barons' Hall, which was octagonal and had a timber roof copied from Crosby Hall, was got up with 'all the upholstery necessary for the occasion' and the walls hung with bits of arras and armour. The Magna Carta window was illuminated from the outside to emphasise the *raison d'etre* for the jollifications.

A dinner was given for 74 people, followed by a ball and supper for 160 guests. Twenty genuine suits of armour were acquired from the Marquess Townshend, whose father had been a president of the Society of Antiquaries and an expert on medieval armour. Metal-workers from Birmingham were hired to repair them, and it was intended that the Duke and Barons should 'equip themselves in these awful habiliments of war; but on examining them they were found in so dilapidated a state that the idea was abandoned'. Instead, the two best sets were hung on dummies to guard the elaborately accoutred 'Baron of Beef'. The Duke made do with his uniform as lord lieutenant of Sussex, which was perhaps just as well, as he had to open the ball with the Marchioness of Stafford and at his age a tight and rusty suit of armour might have induced apoplexy.

A band of Sussex militia played in the 'Minstrels' Gallery' all through dinner, and the more spectacular dishes, such as a whole roast stag, were carried in by retainers in specially designed neo-feudal suits of Lincoln green. According to contemporary accounts, the Duke, incorrigible to the end, did not toast the King but instead drank to the 'pious memory of the Barons who compelled King John to sign Magna Carta'—and to the prettiness of the ladies' maids.

The 11th Duke went out in style. His cousin and successor, Bernard Edward, the 12th Duke, did not live at Arundel nor complete the reconstruction work. He removed the books, carpets and furniture to his own house at Fornham Hall in Suffolk, where he spent the autumn each year, and divided the rest of his time between Norfolk House in London and Worksop Manor which he repaired. But in 1838 Worksop was sold to the Duke of Newcastle who demolished the house and added the land to his own neighbouring estate of Clumber. The family heirlooms from Worksop were sent by boat via the Trent, Humber, North Sea and Channel to Arundel and distributed about the rooms there.

The 13th Duke, as soon as he inherited from his father in 1842, moved into the castle where he set in motion a complete re-decoration and refurnishing under the direction of *the* fashionable interior decorators, G.J. Morant, who had already worked for his father-in-law, the Duke of Sutherland, at Stafford (now Lancaster) House in London. All was ready for Queen Victoria's visit in December 1846. Subsequently the duke employed William Burn to design the impressive (but rather ugly) High Street Lodge in 1851 and various other lodges round the park, as well as to restore the Bevis Tower and to complete the 'Alfred Saloon' as a Billiard Room, removing the Alfred relief (which Charles Stothard the artist had described as 'an exceedingly frightful object') and replacing it with a row of windows. The despised relief was propped up in a corner of the Little Park where odd heads and bits come to light occasionally.

His son, in turn, Henry Granville the 14th Duke, who succeeded in 1856, began a programme of new building at Arundel to the design of M.E. Hadfield of Sheffield in a simple and massive Puginian Gothic manner. The intention was to add a suite of self-contained family rooms, including a large octagonal armoury, at the north end of the east wing, a new kitchen next to the 11th Duke's dining room in the south-west corner, and a completely new gatehouse and chapel between the Barons' Hall and Norman gateway. Only the last

37 Morant table with micromosaic top by the Chevalier Barberi made for the 13th Duke.

was completed at a cost of more than £15,000 when the Duke's premature death occurred in 1860, whereupon the trustees stopped the work and paid Hadfield off. The new chapel, which was intended to sit 200 people, was never used and survived for only 30 years, before being replaced by something far more magnificent as part of the 15th Duke's spectacular reconstruction of the castle after he came of age, and which occupied the whole of the last quarter of the 19th century.

The continuing aim through the various building schemes at Arundel from the 11th Duke to the 15th Duke was to restore a consistently medievalising architectural character to the exterior of the domestic ranges round the quadrangle, and to make the interior into a comfortable modern house as a setting for the large-scale entertaining expected of a late-Georgian or a Victorian duke.

The 11th Duke himself lived a rather raffish bachelor life at Arundel. (His first wife had died in childbirth and his second wife, having succumbed to hereditary mental incapacity, was confined to her own house at Holme Lacey in Herefordshire.) Life at the castle in his time was rough and ready but jolly. Creevey described the conversation at his dinners as being 'in the first style: the subjects infinitely various, from bawdy to the depths of politics' though he did add that there wanted 'a few comforts—such as a necessary, towels, water etc etc to make the thing compleat'. In the 11th Duke's time much of the castle was barely furnished and there was an atmosphere of camping out in the half-finished rooms though he did provide the bedrooms (which he named after the Heralds at the College of Arms: Chester, Lancaster, York and so forth) with large Gothick four posters, a survivor of which now adorns the principal bedroom at Arundel.

Richard Smirke and Samuel Lysons who were guests of the duke in 1811 described the house as it was then. The duke was very generous, providing his carriage so that they could inspect antiquities in the neighbourhood. But they were surprised to find much of the house unfinished and unfurnished. Only the bedrooms were habitable. Dinner was served at 6 o'clock and there were usually ten or twelve guests present—neighbours and clergymen, the conversation being mainly about Sussex, families and property on all of which topics the duke himself was very well informed. It was his practice to consume three or four large glasses of wine at dinner, then to fall asleep, only waking occasionally to fill his glass again and pass the bottle round. At 10 o'clock the company adjourned for tea in the Drawing Room.

In the 12th Duke's time the castle was empty, gloomy and forlorn. Sir Robert Peel, who visited in 1820, found it very depressing: 'We were all greatly disappointed with it, and saw nothing to recompense us for a long drive on a wet day. A very large proportion of the castle is modern, built by the late Duke, who was his own architect. Everything is in bad taste. There are three most expensive paintings on glass, on which the finest colours and the greatest skills have been lavished in representing full-length portraits of the late Duke. In one, he appears as a Baron at the signature of Magna Charta [sic], accompanied by Alderman Combe as a cardinal and Captain Morris, a writer of songs, and one of his drinking companions in some character or other equally appropriate ...The whole scene was a melancholy one. The castle is deserted, as the present Duke dislikes it as a residence. He has removed the books from the Library, and I should think the carpets and furniture from the other rooms. There was not a single fire in any room except the kitchen, and by some coincidence, there were preparations for a funeral in the lodge by which we entered, and in that by which we left the castle'.

Things improved a great deal as soon as the 13th Duke and his wife Charlotte moved in in 1842. She was a Leveson-Gower, the daughter of the Marquess of Stafford, later 1st Duke of Sutherland, who was the richest man in England and lived on a scale to match. When Queen Victoria visited their London home, Stafford House, she quipped to her hostess 'I come from my house to your palace'. The Norfolks were keen that Arundel should not lag behind. Magnificent gold and silver plate was acquired or refurbished, and huge house-parties organised, including usually an annual royal one. In 1844 the Duke and Duchess of Cambridge and the Grand Duke and Duchess of Mecklenburg-Strelitz-Knesbeck were entertained. In 1848 Prince Metternich and the King of Saxony came. In 1849 the Duc de Nemours. Next year there were more French royals, the Comte and Comtesse de Neuilly; in 1853 the Grand Duchess of Russia came to stay and in 1858 Prince Frederick Albert of Prussia. But the apogee of social life at Arundel in the 13th Duke's time was the visit of Queen Victoria and Prince Albert for three days in December 1846. The Duke of Norfolk was Master of the Horse as well as Earl Marshal, and the duchess was one of Queen Victoria's favourite ladies-in-waiting.

The Duke was given two years' notice of the Queen's visit and as the *Illustrated London News* put it: 'during the interval, the noble owner of Arundel has caused the interior of the Castle to be refitted in a style of gorgeous magnificence for the proper reception by England's premier Duke of his Sovereign and her Royal Consort'. Their description of the inside of the castle is worth quoting at length, as it is the most complete account of the rooms as remodelled by the 11th Duke and furnished and decorated by the 13th Duke, prior to the almost total reconstruction of the castle in the last quarter of the 19th century:

Entering the Castle from the court-yard, the visitor is conducted through the hall to a double staircase, with brass railing, which leads to the first floor Corridor, the dimensions of which are 200 feet by 12 feet. The long gallery is crowded with the choicest works of art, including a variety of exquisite specimens of sculpture: among the latter should be particularly mentioned two busts of her Majesty and the Prince Consort, placed at the top of the staircase, and a full length figure of the Lady Adeliza Fitzalan Howard, at the southern extremity of the Corridor; all executed by Francis, in his best style. The Chair of Recognition, used by her Majesty upon the occasion of her coronation, and presented by the Queen to the Duke of Norfolk, as Hereditary Earl Marshal of the Kingdom, is also preserved here. It bears the following inscription:- "The Queen to the Earl Marshal". It is of oak, and the cushion and panel are covered in blue silk velvet.

The effect, on entering this Corridor, is very fine. It is separated from the stair-case by five stone arches, alternately semi-circular and pointed, and enriched with the billet and star Norman mouldings; the capitals of the supporting columns being foliated with the oak, rose vine, and strawberry. The stairs are of stone, and the railings of brass, in the design of intersecting arches.

From this point, a single flight ascends to a handsome triple window, dight with chevron ornament and roses; and flanked by handsome canopied niches, containing busts of Cromwell and Charles the First [*Prince Charles Louis and Charles I* by Dieussart—survivals of the 'Collector' Earl's collection]. Here the stairs again branch in two other divisions to the Upper Corridor, of similar dimensions to the Lower, and fitted in corresponding style.

Returning to the Corridor, from it are entered the Barons' Hall, a superb room, 115 feet in length by 35 in width, and of proportionate height; the roof being formed of Spanish chesnut [sic], in a masterly style of workmanship. This apartment being in an unfinished state, could not be brought into service during her Majesty's visit.

The Banquetting Room was originally the ancient Chapel of the Castle. Over the fireplace in this apartment is a fine portrait of the present Duke of Norfolk, when Earl of Arundel and Surrey, in his robes as a page at the Coronation of George IV, by Hayter. Other portraits of Charles, 11th Duke of Norfolk; of Henry Frederick Howard and Lord Mowbray and Maltravers; of Henry Howard, Earl of Surrey; and of Henry Fitzalan; and of Lord Maltravers, also, grace the walls of this room. The Music Gallery is enriched by exquisite carvings, and furnished with gilt music stands, formerly used in Westminster Abbey. But the most striking effect is produced by a vast window, 27 feet in height, in which are two paintings, on plate-glass, of the Mercy Seat and the Inner Temple. The appointments of this room are truly gorgeous. The candelabra are silver-gilt, the service principally of gold; besides which, there are on the table, a representation in silver, a foot and a half in height, on a pedestal of silver-gilt, of Henry VIII meeting Francis I on the Field of the Cloth of Gold; and a representation of the same size and in the same style of art, of a Norman Crusader and a Saracen in conflict. In addition to this, are six gold coronation cups a foot in depth, and 7 or 8 inches in diameter.

The Great Drawing-Room is upwards of 60 feet in length, and proportionate height. It is lit by four noble windows, commanding a pleasing view of the Vale of the Arun, extending as far as the Miller's Tomb, on Highdown-hill. The walls are hung with paper of gold and green, of the richest design. The furniture is of the most gorgeous description, and comprises buhl and marqueterie cabinets, tables, lounges, &c.; a pianoforte, richly ornamented in gold and white enamel; pier tables of the same descriptions, surmounted by the richest china vases and elaborate clocks. The curtains and chair coverings are of splendid crimson and gold silk damask. The chimney-pieces are of Carrara marble, profusely ornamented and embattled; each bearing, in a centre panel, the Ducal crest, and the Arundel Horse. Mirrors are placed between the windows and at either end of the room, each surmounted by the crests of the various branches of the family, in ornamental decoration, the greater portion of which, embodying the armorial bearings, autographs, and insignia of the family, are stated to have been executed from designs furnished by the ladies of the family. The portraits in this room include those of Thomas Duke of Norfolk, by Holbein; of Henry Howard, the Sixth Duke; of Thomas Howard, Earl of Arundel, the celebrated collector; of Alethia Talbot, Countess of Arundel and Surrey; of Mary Fitzalan, Duchess of Norfolk; of Ludovick Stuart Duke of Richmond; and, above all in historical interest, of John Howard, first Duke of Norfolk of the Howard family, the celebrated "Jocky" of Shakesperian [*sic*] celebrity.

The Small or Ante Drawing-Room is connected with the room just described and furnished in similar style: it contains several paintings, among which are an original cabinet painting of Richard III, for which the Duke of Norfolk has refused 3000 guineas; of Charles I and Henrietta Maria, by Vandyke; and Mary and Elizabeth of York. Here is also deposited the original full-length portrait of Christina, Duchess of Milan, painted by Holbein [now in the National Gallery, London] at the command of Henry VIII, and who, it will be remembered, returned to him, on the solicitation of her hand, the memorable answer, that *had she more than one head it should be at his service*. Of more immediate interest, however, are three portraits of her Majesty Queen Victoria, at the respective ages of four, ten, and nineteen years, all painted by Fowler. Here, also, is a fine portrait of the present Duke of Norfolk, by Pickersgill. On the table is a copy of a matchless work by Rubens, relating to some members of the Howard Family.

On the opposite side of the Corridor is the Library, 120 feet in length by 24 in width. It is entirely fitted with mahogany, exquisitely veined. The bookcases and reading galleries are supported by fifteen columns, wrought out of the finest solid mahogany, highly polished. The ceiling is formed out of the same material, enriched with exquisite carvings of fruit and foliage, &c. The library contains, in addition to a rare collection

38 *The Drawing Room as redecorated for Queen Victoria's visit in 1846.*

of manuscripts, about 14,000 volumes. The draperies are of rich crimson velvet, and the effect of the whole is rich; though we scarcely admire the employment in a Gothic building of mahogany, which has been known in this country but a century and a quarter.

A second staircase leads to another Corridor of equal extent with that just described, and in the same manner studded with picture and works of art. In the eastern wing of this Corridor is the suite of apartments which has been prepared for her Majesty and her Royal Consort. It consists of six rooms, furnished in a style of regal splendour, every item throughout the suite being new for the occasion. The draperies and furniture coverings are of the richest silk damask, in white enamel and gold.-Her Majesty's Dressing-Room contains some choice bits of the scenery of Arundel, painted by Copley Fielding; and a fire-screen, beautifully worked with the Norfolk arms.-The Queen's Private Sitting-Room has a matchless buhl cabinet and writing-desk; several

portraits of the juvenile branches of the Royal Family; and two unrivalled specimens of Prout's pencil: "Munich" and "Milan".-The Royal Breakfast-Room displays a series of etchings by the present Duchess of Norfolk; they are much admired for freedom and beauty of touch.

The Royal State Bed has been built expressly for this Visit: it is of highly artistic design, with lavish brilliancy of decoration. It is of white and gold, and richly carved throughout, surmounted by a gorgeous canopy, in the centre of which rises a dome, formed of gold-coloured satin, interlaced and looped with thick rope of gold. In the corners of the interior of the canopy, appear the letters "V.R.," in gilt carving, laid upon and relieved by white satin. The head pillars which support the canopy are beautifully carved; and the twisted reeds of the upper part of the columns are intertwined with strings of pearls, producing a remarkably pleasing and elegant effect. The cornice which encloses the canopy is ornamented at the angles with carved Imperial crowns; and in the centre of the sides and front appears the Horse of Arundel, with an oak-branch in his mouth, and supported by a series of elaborate scroll-work. The head of the Bedstead is beautifully rayed in gold-coloured silk, and the head-board is covered with crimson brocade, surmounted by the Royal Arms, exquisitely carved; together with a profusion of the flowers and leaves of the rose, thistle, and shamrock. The foot-board is also richly carved, and surmounted by the Ducal Arms, beautifully chiselled, and richly gilt; the foot-rails, &c., are literally covered with carved and gilt oak-leaves; and the bases are of heavy crimson-silk bullion fringe, interspersed with gold-coloured silk hangings. The draperies of the Bed are of rich crimson and gold brocade, lined with gold-coloured satin; the shaped valances being looped with massive silk-rope tassels, and trimmed with gold bullion fringe. Altogether, the State Bed has a most splendid effect. The window-curtains correspond with the Bed. In this chamber, too, is a richly-carved screen, worked with the Sutherland arms. The walls throughout this suite are hung with paper richly and tastefully gilt; and, in addition to the pictures already described, present several splendid mirrors and works of art. The State Bed and Furniture of the Royal Bed and Dressing Rooms have been designed and executed by Mr. Morant, of 91, New Bond-street, and they are in artistical taste rarely equalled.

One detail which the *Illustrated London News* did not comment on was the heating of the castle in December which had been a worry to the duchess for 'the Galleries here are so impossible to warm'. But as she later told Miss Burdett Coutts, 'We have fortunately procured a great alleviation to that evil in Joyce's Stoves, a thing like a flowerpot which by the greatest good fortune my sister had seen at Raby Castle, just in time to a day for us to procure some of them'.

The Queen and the Prince Consort came on the Royal Yacht from Osborne, then across country via Chichester in a carriage procession with a military escort. In Arundel town, where all the houses had been loyally decorated, the royal party was met by the Mayor, Mr Howard Gibbon (one of the 11th Duke's many illegitimate children) and a line up of the school children. *The Morning Post* gave a description of the royal arrival at the castle on Tuesday, 1 December:

As the royal carriage entered the Castle gate, two royal standards were run up on either side the same; and as it passed into the quadrangle the Duke's flag was lowered from the summit of the keep, and the British flag hoisted

39   *Bracelet with miniature of Queen Victoria by Henry Bone given to Lady Mary Fitzalan Howard (Foley).*

in its stead. At the same moment a most brilliant illumination in gas, extending entirely across the keep, burst forth in great brilliancy, exhibiting in colossal letters these words–"Welcome Victoria and Albert".

On alighting, her Majesty was received in the entrance hall by the Duchess of Norfolk, whom she most affectionately greeted. The Duchess of Sutherland, Lady John Russell, and others of the circle assembled at the Castle, were also in attendance to welcome her Majesty.

As her Majesty entered the Castle, the band of the Yeomanry Cavalry played the national anthem, a salute of twenty-one guns being fired at the same moment from a battery stationed in the Home Park.

Her Majesty was first conducted to the state drawing-room, and having exchanged courtesies with the guests therein, shortly after retired to her private apartment.'

After dinner on the first night where 'the table presented a gorgeous display of plate. The dessert service was of gold', there was a fireworks display and the castle and town were illuminated. On Wednesday, after a walk in the grounds 'full of beautiful evergreens, which made Albert extremely jealous for Osborne' (as the Queen noted in her diary) the men went shooting. After lunch, the Duke showed the Queen the dairy, the deer park and the owls in the keep which she thought 'very wise looking but at the same time rather formidable'. At dinner, there was a different display of plate and, as well as the house party, the Bishop of Chichester and Colonel Wyndham from Petworth also attended. Afterwards there was a concert of 'Ethiopian singers' in the Library whom the Queen thought 'though laughable ... rather tiresome'. Refreshments were served in the Dining Room and everybody retired at half-past eleven.

The following day, the royal party went over to Petworth in the morning to admire the paintings

40 *Portrait of Queen Victoria by William Fowler, commissioned by the 13th Duke for her visit.*

which the Queen considered beautiful but 'badly arranged'. After a late lunch at Arundel, the Queen visited the Fitzalan Chapel and the greenhouse 'which is so nice and beautifully kept, as everything here'. After dinner, again with different plate and this evening with Lord and Lady March from Goodwood as the extra guests, a conjuror performed tricks and then there was dancing, concluding with 'a very merry country dance' which the Queen led with the duke. The royal party left at 10 o'clock on the morning of Friday, 4 December, the Queen having enjoyed herself and liked Arundel which reminded her of Windsor with its keep, collegiate chapel and pretty views over the surrounding hilly wooded country: 'The ruined keep is wonderfully like the position of the Round Tower at Windsor, and then there are 2 entrances to the courtyard, equivalent to our 2 and the Collegiate, now Parish, Church stands as St George's Chapel does, with the town below—all in keeping. Unfortunately the Castle has not been restored in a good style, by Duke Charles, the last but one, and Saxon and Gothic architecture are mixed'.

Considering the almost universal disparagement of the 11th Duke's architecture, it is hardly surprising that Henry, the 15th Duke had so few qualms in sweeping nearly all of it away, and replacing it with something infinitely more solid, serious and scholarly.

Chapter IV

The Modern Castle

Henry, 15th Duke of Norfolk, came of age in December 1868 after a minority during which his trustees had nurtured estates in Norfolk, Sussex, Surrey and Yorkshire, as well as a substantial portion of Sheffield and a slice of the Strand in London. He embarked immediately on a lavish building programme, calling in Charles Nosotti to refurbish Norfolk House in London and Joseph Aloysius Hansom to erect a cathedral-scale Catholic church at Arundel, which is now the Cathedral of the Catholic diocese of Arundel and Brighton. The plans for this church (originally dedicated to St Philip Neri and now Our Lady and St Philip Howard) were drawn up by Hansom in 1869 and

building began in 1870, the contractors being George Myers & Sons of Lambeth. The foundation stone was laid on 7 June 1870 by a Benedictine monk, Dom William Placid Morris, Bishop of Troy *ex partibus*, and work was completed in 1873. The cost of the building (excluding the high altar, stations of the cross, vestments and plate, which the duke and his family gave to the church piecemeal in succeeding years) was £65,000. The official opening by Cardinal Manning took place on 1 July 1873 at a magnificent service with a large congregation including nearly all the canons of Southwark Cathedral and the Fathers of the London Oratory. Pontifical High Mass was sung

41 Arundel Cathedral, 1868-74, designed by J. A. Hansom.

42 *Arundel Cathedral interior, with flower carpet for Corpus Christi processtion.*

by the Bishop of Southwark with music by Hummel and Anfossi, an orchestra and organ and, as the recessional, the march from *Tannhäuser* by Wagner. The choir of Brompton Oratory came down to Arundel specially for the occasion.

The finest feature of the church is the stained glass in the transepts, sanctuary and western rose window made by Hardman & Powell of Birmingham, and the elaborate stone carving by Farmer & Brindley. The stations of the cross are by Boulton & Sons of Cheltenham. A baldachino proposed for the High Altar never materialised and as a result the east end of the church lacks the intended focus. It looks its best at the annual feast of Corpus Christi when a procession of the Blessed Sacrament takes place from the cathedral to the castle where there is benediction in the quadrangle, according to the tradition started by Duke Henry in 1874, and the nave floor is covered with a patterned mosaic of flowers on the Italian model.

At the castle itself there was no doubt that the young duke would continue the reconstruction begun by his father but halted by the latter's premature death in 1860. He could not, however, make up his mind about an architect, and rather surprisingly seems at first to have considered Matthew Digby Wyatt, who in the 1860s was working on various Sussex houses. But Wyatt was not a Catholic and the duke wished to provide employment for his co-religionists. In the end, he chose Charles Alban Buckler (1824-1904).

Buckler was a Catholic convert and scion of the Oxford antiquarian dynasty. His father, John Chessell Buckler, was the famous topographical draughtsman, author of such works as *Remarks upon Wayside Chapels*, and architect of Costessy Hall in Norfolk. It seems likely that Buckler came to the notice of the Howards through Minna Duchess of Norfolk, for whom he designed St Peter's Church, Shoreham, in 1874. When he was given the commission for reconstructing Arundel, Buckler conscientiously made a study of other old Sussex castles, preparing sketches of details at Bodiam, Bramber, Pevensey, Lewes and other ancient sites in the county.

Buckler was a characteristic Victorian architect, deeply religious and devoted to the study of medieval art and liturgy. He inherited the artistic skills of his father and grandfather, and his work always reaches a high standard. His country houses include additions to Sutton Place and Newstead Abbey. He was one of the few 19th-century Catholic architects who tried to create a medieval glamour which was quiet, scholarly and English; his work is very different from the gutsy vulgarity of George Goldie or E.W. Pugin.

Arundel is above all a client's building. The duke approved every detail, from the colours of paint to the silhouette of a merlon. When in London he telegraphed his decisions to the clerk of works. Buckler sent a constant stream of sketches and drawings for his opinion. The duke chose subjects for stained glass and sculpture, and approved the outline to towers and chimneys only after variants in cut-out boards had been hoisted to the skyline for comparison. He was also responsible for many practical suggestions, such as the use of gun-metal rather than iron for the casements to prevent corrosion.

The craftsmanship is first-rate throughout. Like many Victorian architectural clients, from Peabody to the Midland Railway, the duke wanted his new house to last at least 1,000 years. Arundel is amazingly well built, and designed so as to require little maintenance. There is nothing external that needs to be painted, and the ashlar stonework is so finely laid that it hardly requires pointing. The roof is entirely covered in lead. The foundations of the south front are of concrete and 50 ft deep.

As we have seen, the house that Buckler was called upon to reconstruct in the 1870s was a hotch-potch. On the south and east sides it incorporated substantial 12th-century remains. Grafted onto this was the gothick house designed by the 11th Duke, but left incomplete on his death in 1815. On the west side were Hadfield's unfinished additions for the 14th Duke. The 15th Duke was keen to preserve the old fabric, as well as the convenient layout, of the 11th Duke's state rooms. It was only on the west side of the castle, therefore, that Buckler was allowed to demolish the incomplete Regency and Hadfield work, and to rebuild from the foundations upwards, though even here the 12th-century curtain wall which had survived the 11th Duke's reconstruction was retained and refaced as the west wall of the new Barons' Hall. This retention of old fabric explains the main defect of the design, namely the quadrangle's south and east façades, which seem too even, have too many windows and are lacking in warmth and movement. This is because they are largely a refacing only.

Where Buckler had a mainly free hand, in the west wing, he was able to contrive a powerful

43 *The east wing reconstructed in 1877.*

composition of geometrical masses in which cylindrical towers 130 ft. high, the square projection of the kitchen and the high, triangular section of the Barons' Hall roof contribute to a highly impressive whole. The distant silhouette, too, is entirely satisfying, thanks to the variety and disposition of the turrets and chimneystacks.

Building began in 1877 with the addition of a new kitchen on the west side, the remodelling of the Drawing Room in the south range and family rooms at the north end of the east wing. This followed Hadfield's proposals in 1859, but the architecture was now more austere and bold. The exterior was faced with Doulting and Whitby stone towards the quadrangle, with some flintwork on the outer elevations. The contractor was P.J. McManus of Hammersmith.

The new kitchen block contained a scullery, three larders, a pastry room, a cook's room, a fish larder, a vegetable room and staff lavatories, in addition to the kitchen itself. Its construction was largely fireproof, with 'rolled iron' (steel) joists, and the interior was lined with Keen's cement and

Minton tiles. The domestic arrangements at Arundel were of the most advanced character. It is partly the combination of modern technology and medieval antiquarianism which makes the house so fascinating.

A significant aspect of the late 19th-century work at Arundel was the advanced nature of the services and fittings, which were provided on a truly American scale. Arundel was one of the first English country houses to be built with electric light, sophisticated plumbing—including eight bathrooms and 65 water closets—integral fire-fighting equipment, service lifts and central heating. The wash basins and baths were supplied by Dent & Hellyer and the hydraulic powered luggage lift by George Johnson in 1897. Central heating was installed from 1879 onwards and Buckler designed the handsome gunmetal radiators, or 'heating coils' as he called them, which are still in use, although the old coal-fired boilers have been changed to North Sea gas. The radiators were made by James Slater of Holborn, who also supplied the electric bell system.

Hill and Hey provided a patent 'siphon ventilator' for the kitchen in 1881. The fire-fighting equipment was devised and supplied by J.C. Merriweather, who described it in his book *Fire Protection of Mansions* (1884). It is worth quoting his own description verbatim:

The fire extinguishing arrangements at Arundel Castle are as follows:- In the first place there is a steam fire engine, capable of throwing upwards of 300 gallons per minute, and always ready at a moment's notice; in addition to this is a manual engine, and about a dozen hydrants with hose attached, in the different parts of the interior of the castle. Within a short distance of the castle is a large lake, from which the water supply is derived; adjoining the lake is the engine-house, containing a large water wheel and two pumping engines, the latter being worked by the water wheel, with surplus water from the lake. The water is forced through a five-inch rising main to a height of about 150 feet into a large storage tank, which is called the fire tank, and which contains 400,000 gallons; an overflow pipe from this supplies a second tank containing 200,000 gallons more, which supplies the castle and various hydrants in the town with water for domestic purposes. These tanks are situated about a quarter of a mile from the Castle, and are at a sufficient elevation to carry the water by gravitation to some fifteen feet or so above the castle roof. The water is conveyed from the tanks to the castle by two cast-iron mains, a four-inch for the domestic supply and a five-inch for the exclusive supply of the steam fire engine; both mains, however, are available in case of fire.

As well as the hydrants disposed around the castle, there were also fire alarm bells in the little gothic hutches, one or two of which still survive.

44   *The west wing under construction in 1894.*

it is a jolt to compare this sum with the cost of the splendidly carved chimneypiece in the Drawing Room, for which Thomas Earp, the doyen of architectural sculptors, charged a mere £150. The lighting system was devised by Arthur Phillips, 'electrical engineer', and executed by the Brush Electrical Engineering Company Ltd of Loughborough in 1891-99. A (half-timbered) generator house was built near the stables to contain two Victoria Steam Dynamos, each of 90 h.p., powered by a 'Lancashire type' boiler. Wires in iron conduits were laid underground for a distance of 800 yd. to the castle, where they fed 1,000 lamps. The oak bosses for the light switches were designed by Buckler, as were the electroliers in the main rooms. In the east wing the internal wiring had to be installed retrospectively, which the clerk of works described as 'simply ... butchery', but it was included in the south and west wings as part of the 1890s contract.

The initial building contract was completed by 1881, and soon after that McManus was paid off, because the duke thought his 10 per cent commission was excessive, particularly as Buckler only charged 5 per cent. Rattee and Kett of

46   Detail of window frame and catch made of gun metal.

The arrangements for the domestic water supply were as carefully considered; it was also piped *gratis* by the duke to serve the town. A (Norman) pump house with two steam engines lifted the water through a 5in. rising main from Swanbourne Lake, 150ft. below the castle, to a 200,000 gallon tank beside the cricket field a quarter of a mile away. Thence a 4in. domestic main conveyed the water, by gravity, to the castle. Nearly all the principal bedrooms were provided with connecting water closets. The four principal guest bedrooms had their own bathrooms, as had the duke's own apartment and the nursery. Three separate sets of gentlemen's lavatories with stone-vaulted cubicles and magnificent washbasins of Purbeck marble were contrived on the ground floor.

The ultimate wonder was, however, the electric light, which cost a truly staggering £36,169 16s. 2d. This throws comparative prices into perspective. Looking back from a world where technology is cheap and craftsmanship expensive,

45 (left)   The 15th Duke's house, designed by C. A. Buckler.

47   The Chapel with Purbeck columns and lavish carving.

48 *The Scullery, part of the kitchen block, 1877.*

49 *The Drawing Room (1877) in the time of the 15th Duke.*

Cambridge were taken on as the main contractors. It was intended to begin the new west wing in 1880, but personal tragedy intervened and delayed construction for nearly 10 years.

In 1877 the duke married Lady Flora Abney-Hastings, and a son, Philip, was born two years later. The boy, however, was blind and epileptic; he never developed beyond the mental age of a baby, although he lived till he was 21. The duchess, too, succumbed to an incurable disease, and died, aged only 34, in 1887. While his wife was ill, the duke suspended building. But after her death he began again on an even larger scale, as solace in his bereavement. (He did not remarry until 1904, after his son died.)

The south range, including the façade to the quadrangle, and the projecting Dining Room, on the site of the medieval chapel, was begun in 1891 and completed in 1898. The west wing, containing the new chapel and the Barons' Hall, was begun in 1893 and completed in 1899. Buckler retired in 1901. The foundation stone of the chapel was laid in February 1894 by the Archbishop of Southwark. During all this decade, the quadrangle was a builders' yard, filled with huts, a crane, scaffolding and piles of materials. Between 150 and 300 workmen were employed on an almost permanent basis.

Although unmistakably Victorian in its hardness of finish and surprisingly tough details—short, stumpy columns seemingly crushed by the weight of masonry above, massive plain corbels, string courses abruptly cut off, sharp, unmoulded tracery and brobdingnagian geometry—the design of Arundel was also a scholarly exercise.

Hours can be spent tracing the more *recherché* sources. The duke owned books on gothic architecture by Viollet-le-Duc, Seroux d'Agincourt, Rickman, Pugin, Street, Ruskin and Scott. The kitchen gateway is based on an arch at Glastonbury; the hall and drawing-room windows are copied from the King's Hall at Winchester; the carved Crucifixion over the north gateway in the quadrangle is inspired by a stained-glass panel at Le Mans Cathedral. The chimneys are derived from New College. The hall roof is a compilation from the Guesten Hall at Worcester. The hooded fireplaces and iron curtain cranes come from Viollet-le-Duc. The chapel is an imaginative reconstruction of Henry III's vanished Lady Chapel at Westminster Abbey.

50 *The iron kitchen stoves supplied by Parkinson of London and Birmingham.*

The heraldry is the fruit of research by Buckler in the College of Arms. It permeates the architecture in carvings, stained glass, tiles, ironwork and painted decorations. Abstracted details, such as the Hastings manche, serve as keyholes, and Fitzalan acorns and oak leaves embellish door hinges. Ducal strawberry leaves, Plantagenet broom pods, and Howard cross crosslets fitchée enliven the stained glass borders of windows. The variety of detail is mesmerising. Every window has a different pattern of leadwork, every door a different type of hinge and keyhole; nothing is repeated or mass-produced. Large-scale working drawings were provided for everything, and survive in their hundreds.

The truly impressive aspect of this is that Buckler prepared all these himself, without any help. He explained proudly to the duke, when he retired in 1901: 'It is true that my dear Father and I did not employ clerks or incur the responsibility of pupils. We prepared our own designs and supplied the architectural details and the result was satisfactory'.

Although the overall scheme for the castle had been devised in the 1870s, some interesting changes were made in the course of execution. Buckler's original plan had been to place the dining room on the quadrangle side of the south wing and to restore the old medieval chapel to use. The three tall lancet windows overlooking the river were designed for the chapel but were retained when the room became the dining room instead. A proposed new gatehouse on the west, originally intended to serve as the main entrance to the

51 *Typical oak cupboard designed by C. A. Buckler for the servants' quarters.*

52 *Hydraulic motor for the lift, 1890.*

Barons' Hall, was eliminated and the Norman gateway brought back into use as the principal approach to the castle. This enabled a larger and more impressive chapel to be constructed. The total cost of the successive building contracts between 1877 and 1904 amounted to the enormous sum of £570,377 17s. 10d. according to a note compiled for the duke by the Arundel agent in 1908. This included £15,166 7s. 5d. for the water supply and drains, and £21,559 5s. 11d. for making the new Mill Road.

The duke was keen to preserve all that remained of the Norman castle, and the architect and builder had instructions not to damage any ancient features that might be revealed in the course of work. The uncovering of Henry II's blocked windows in the outer wall of the Drawing Room was a great thrill and they were carefully restored. The local newspaper, *The West Sussex Gazette*, described their rediscovery in July 1879 in between details of the grass crop and other local news: 'In the work of restoration of the old baronial residence of Arundel castle, a very interesting discovery has been made. In clearing the surface of the south front, for inserting the new Drawing Room windows, a very pretty little Norman arch or window is discovered, close to the eastern extremity of the south front. It is quite a little gem for the antiquary; and we doubt not that the Duke of Norfolk, who possesses much archaeological taste, is delighted at the incident. The discovery will surprise many, for it is generally supposed that the present castle was comparatively modern, being erected on the old Norman foundations; but now it is seen that a good portion of the superstructure of the Norman castle was preserved; and this little arch appears to be the same that we find in a sketch of the Old Arundel castle in Tierney's *History*—the walls of which are popularly supposed to have been demolished.'

When it came to the restoration of the keep in 1905-6, after Buckler's retirement, the duke took steps to preserve as much of the old fabric as possible and the work was done conservatively under the direction of John Morley of Cambridge, an expert on old castles. The curtain walls and outlying towers had been restored under Buckler's direction in 1901-2. He had used a surviving section near the keep as a model for re-instating the battlements, but had completed the ruined towers imaginatively; originally, those in the curtain wall of the north

53 *Fire alarm bell, part of Merryweather's protection system.*

54 *Victorian pipework in the basement.*

55 *Victorian bath and washbasin supplied by Dent & Hellyer.*

bailey had been open backed, like those which survive at Framlingham.

In many ways, the interior of Buckler's castle is its best feature. It is remarkably ingenious and consistent in its adaptation of mid-13th century architecture to late 19th-century domestic requirements. Unlike the other great 19th-century castle-houses, Windsor and Alnwick, Arundel is as full-bloodedly gothic inside as out. From the butler's pantry to the nursery bathroom, everything is in the purest 13th-century style. Buckler and the duke did not flinch from consistency, quite the reverse. They obviously derived enormous fun from finding medieval sources for electroliers, picture hooks, kitchen cupboards and even a billiard table, although Buckler's design for a gothic carpet does not seem to have been executed.

56 *Gunmetal radiator designed by Buckler, made by Slater of Holborn.*

Pugin is supposed to have died calling for a gothic pudding. He would have approved of Arundel; and much that Buckler achieved would not have been possible without his influence, for many of the firms and materials used in its embellishment were Puginian in origin and inspiration, notably Hardman of Birmingham for metalware and stained glass, Minton for encaustic tiles and Crace for fabrics. In its excellent craftsmanship and consistent use of mid-13th-century sources, Arundel is Pugin's ideal made solidly manifest.

The interior of the castle is, however, more complex than this assertion might suggest. For though the architecture is archaeologically correct in detail, the actual plan of the state rooms is grandly Georgian, and derives from the evolution of the house in the course of the 18th century.

The 11th Duke had kept the bones of the plan when he gothicked the castle. He converted the 16th-century long gallery into a library and created a 100 yd. axial sequence through it, from the incomplete Alfred Saloon at the north end (site of the Billiard Room) through an ante-library to the small drawing room (now the duke's sitting room) in the corner tower. Another axial sequence was continued at right-angles along the south front, through the large drawing room, small dining room or anteroom to the large dining room in the shell of the secularised former chapel. At the same time, the south wing was doubled in width by the addition of suites of bedrooms on the north side of the gallery, facing the quadrangle.

The 11th Duke had rebuilt the west wing to contain a great hall (on the late-medieval site) and chapel. The 15th Duke and Buckler retained this basic plan, which gives the interior a splendidly logical sequence of state rooms, rather than the picturesque jumble of medieval spaces that might perhaps have been expected within so severe a castellated exterior.

As well as reconstructing nearly all the 11th Duke's interior, apart from the Library, and totally rebuilding the chapel and Barons' Hall, the 15th Duke also refurnished much of it. Morant's upholstered furniture must have seemed rather dowdy when it was 40 years old, and while the 15th Duke greatly admired the splendid 18th-century furniture from Worksop which he deployed to advantage, there was not enough of it to fill the much-enlarged castle; many of the rooms of which

57 *Stained glass by Hardman in Barons' Hall with medieval family history.*

are enormous by any standards. The 1890s Barons' Hall, for instance, is 133 ft. long and 50 ft. high. The chapel is 78 ft. long and over 30 ft. high. The Picture Gallery is 192 ft. long (as is the passage below and the top gallery above), the Dining Room 60 ft. long and 34 ft. high and the Drawing Room 55 ft. long and 25 ft. wide, and many of the other rooms are commensurate in scale.

Throughout the 1880s Duke Henry bought discerningly and on a large scale, using as his agent Charles Davis, a Bond Street dealer, who bid on the duke's behalf at Christies as well as negotiating with other dealers. Gothic furniture was not available in suitable quantities (though the duke did acquire some late-medieval woodwork, including a rare 15th-century carved Flemish altarpiece, and smaller objects including a 15th-century Venetian ivory casket); so he bought largely continental pieces from the 16th to the 18th centuries, the scale and elaborate craftsmanship of which gave them an honorary gothic character and helped to enliven the somewhat austere, scholarly architecture of the new rooms. These included a large series of French and Flemish carved oak and walnut cabinets and tables with which the duke furnished the Barons' Hall, and a number of ivory-inlaid chairs, tables and coffers, some of which today are in the Armoury and others scattered around the principal rooms.

Many of these things came from well-known earlier antiquarian collections which were being dispersed in the late 19th century. The best pieces in the armoury assembled by Duke Henry, with its fine polearms and swords, came from the Brett Collection while others were acquired for him by Charles Davis in France. Some of the furniture and pictures were acquired at the Beresford Hope sale at Christies in May 1886. As well as furniture, carvings and armour, Duke Henry also bought a number of important early panel paintings including three Italian altarpieces, several Flemish triptychs and the only example in England of the rare School of Avignon.

As well as reconstructing the castle, the 15th Duke also carried out massive improvements to its setting. A private cricket ground was laid out in the Little Park in 1894. The private garden in the north bailey was replanted by Gertrude Jekyll. The approaches were also redesigned. By part-exchange, after long negotiations, the duke acquired the ancient Burgess Brooks, the fields to the south of the castle which had belonged to the town council since the Middle Ages, which were vital for preserving the castle foreground. This enabled him to close Mill Lane which ran immediately underneath the south front; so close that the oaths of carters driving their wagons past could be clearly heard in summer through the open windows of the Drawing Room. In its place the duke created the present Mill Road, which sweeps in an elegant curve further away from the castle. The duke planted this handsomely as an avenue of limes and gave it to the town council. A new Lower Lodge was erected in Mill Road to Buckler's design, and a carefully engineered meandering drive was contrived through the castle grounds, where at last, after a century of clearing away urban encroachments, complete privacy was now ensured. The 11th Duke had diverted the London Road to the south of St Nicholas's Church and converted the medieval Marygate (once one of the town gates)

into an ornament of the castle grounds. The 12th Duke had built a new Town Hall in Maltravers Street so that he could remove the town council from the vestry of the Fitzalan Chapel. The 13th Duke had demolished all the buildings (which belonged to him) at the top of the High Street, to build William Burn's High Street Lodge and the adjoining castellated wall. He had also tried to move Mill Lane but had failed at that stage. Now Duke Henry had succeeded in securing this final bit of the jigsaw.

This may sound rebarbative but, while creating a suitably spacious setting for the castle, the dukes were not keeping people out. Far from it. Running hand in hand with the restoration of the castle from the late 18th to the late 19th century was the regular opening of the place to the public. What is often thought to be a very modern phenomenon— the 'stately home' which is partly the private house of a great family and partly a national monument open to visitors—has been the case at Arundel for the last 200 years.

In 1800 the keep, gatehouse and grounds were opened every day by the 11th Duke. But from 1805 this was regularised to two days a week all the year round, with tickets acquired beforehand from the *Norfolk Arms* in the High Street. The main rooms, too, were opened one day a week in the summer towards the end of the 11th Duke's lifetime. Although it was largely empty, the castle continued to be open in the 12th Duke's time and a first guide book was printed for visitors in 1817 which went into several later editions. At that time visitors were said to come from all over Britain. The park too was freely open to the public from the moment that it was created in 1790.

The 13th Duke closed the private part of the house but continued to open the grounds, the keep, the Norman gatehouse and the model dairy, erected to the design of Robert Abraham in 1844, two days a week, Monday and Friday, throughout the year. He also opened the flower garden, as the following quotation from the *Horticultural Journal* in 1854 makes clear:

Arundel Castle Gardens.–In addition to the annual opening of these gardens and grounds to the inhabitants of the town and their friends, his Grace the Duke of Norfolk has kindly granted this season another privilege of a novel character, viz., the illumination of the flower gardens, which are now in great perfection. Nearly 3000 lamps were in use on the ocasion, and being disposed in straight and drapery lines on the terraces with festoons, wreaths, and arches on the arcades and walls, together with a liberal admixture in the flower beds and by the fountain, the effect of the whole was very striking. Upwards of 3000 visitors promenaded in the gardens from half-past 8 to half-past 10 o'clock. The duke's brass band was stationed on the terraces. It is gratifying to add that not the slightest injury was done, and an excellent tone pervaded the gathering. G. McEwen, August 22.

The coming of the new coastal (Brighton-Portsmouth) railway to Ford, two miles away, in 1846 increased the numbers of visitors from London and further afield. A special new guide book, *A Day in Arundel*, was published by George Hillier in 1847.

Many can make a short holiday, to whom a distant trip is impracticable ... with that most remarkable feature of the present age, the increased rapidity of travelling, remote places are brought nearer to each other and distance is but little heeded; therefore to you who are planning such recreation—to the lover of nature and our national antiquities, to those who will draw pleasure from every wholesome source—I say, take your place on the South Coast Railway, and assure yourself that there are few places more worthy of a visit, than the ancient Town and Castle of Arundel'—just what the castle comptroller says today.

There was a regular omnibus service from the station at Ford to Arundel where 'the great point of attraction [is] the residence of England's premier duke'. A new guide book to the castle was published in 1851 at the time of the Great Exhibition, as it was thought that some of the visitors to London for that might wish to benefit from a day-trip to Sussex. From June 1856 till the 1930s, visitors' books were kept with the signatures and addresses of those who came to the castle. In 1857 there were 1,102 tourists; in 1858, 3,238; in 1859, 7,394. In the 1860s the numbers averaged between 10 and 14 thousand a year, though 16,693 came in 1864, the year after the station was opened in Arundel itself on the new line from Horsham. Figures kept at around these levels for the rest of the century. In 1888 there were 11,280 visitors and in 1890, 14,520. Some of the visitors were from Sussex or London but overall they were very mixed, both socially and geographically: Ireland, India, Dieppe, Australia and Northamptonshire being given as addresses. Many of them, judging from their domiciles in Islington or Camden Town,

were lower middle class or 'respectable artisans' on family outings. But there were also sea captains and imperial civil servants on leave, groups of archaeologists, and vegetarians, French counts and Scottish peeresses, and even Napoleon III in exile, who came by train from Bognor; he would have wished particularly to compare the 15th Duke's work with his own massive reconstruction of Pierrefonds to the design of Viollet-le-Duc. Arundel is actually better; but did the deposed French emperor think so?

In 1900, after the completion of the major part of his remodelling of the castle, the 15th Duke decided to re-open the main rooms to the public as they had been in the early 19th century. The old keep and dairy continued to be shown free of charge (tickets from the *Norfolk Arms*) on Monday and Wednesday afternoons throughout the year. The interior of the castle and the Fitzalan Chapel were shown on Wednesday only with an admission charge of one shilling each (no deduction for children), tickets being sold at the High Street lodge. The proceeds, after a percentage had been deducted and given to the clerk on duty at the lodge and to the castle servants who showed visitors round, were divided 'as the Duke should decide between Chichester Infirmary, Brighton County Hospital, The Brighton Eye Hospital, St Philip's Club and the Victoria Institute'. These opening arrangements survived until the Second World War.

Duke Henry married in 1904 Gwendolen Constable-Maxwell, the daughter of the 11th Lord Herries (whose title she later inherited in her own right). They had three daughters and a son, Bernard Marmaduke who inherited the dukedom at the age of nine when his father died in 1917. Throughout the 1920s and into the 1930s life at Arundel continued much as before the First World War, with large family parties attended by Maxwell and Howard cousins throughout the year, for cricket in summer and shoots in the winter. Christmas was always spent at Arundel, when there was a big party in the Barons' Hall for the staff and estate, and the children used to put on a play in the Library each year, which they devised and acted themselves.

Duchess Gwendolen, who was extremely energetic, also used the castle for her own charities, especially the Red Cross of which she was chairman of the Sussex branch. Concerts and other events were held regularly in the Barons' Hall to raise

58 *Restoration of the Keep, 1905.*

money for this and other good causes. The Barons' Hall, which has fine acoustics, has always been used for concerts. One of the first performances of Elgar's *Dream of Gerontius* had taken place there in 1906, organised by the duchess, with Gervase Elwes as the tenor, the Sheffield Choir and the Queen's Hall Orchestra conducted by Henry Wood.

Following Duke Bernard's marriage to Lavinia Strutt (the daughter of Lord Belper) in 1937, considerable changes were put in hand at Arundel, aimed at modernising the castle and making it more comfortable, while a racing stable was established on the estate. A new laundry and additional bathrooms were installed. A tennis court and swimming pool were contrived in the north bailey, and many of the bedrooms and subsidiary rooms lightened by painting the stonework white and close-carpeting the floors. The following year, following the sale of Norfolk House, the best furniture, pictures and the muniments from there were brought down to Sussex and installed in the

castle, but were hardly unpacked because the programme of improvements was suddenly interrupted by the outbreak of the Second World War.

The castle, like many other large houses in Britain, was occupied by troops; waves of English, American and Canadian soldiers passing through between June 1940 and July 1945. One bathroom was reserved for the exclusive use on Saturdays of WAAFs from Ford Airfield. The keep was an important lookout post in the coastal defences, manned by the Royal Observer Corps, and during the Battle of Britain the Home Guard mounted a night piquet on the South Tower. In various ways, therefore, the castle for five years played a proper military role which the 15th Duke and his architect, C.A. Buckler, could hardly have envisaged in the 1870s when they devoted so much attention to perfecting its 13th-century fortifications.

The East Wing was taken over by the army in June 1940 and was continuously occupied by different units till July 1945. The regiments who occupied the castle during these five years included 7th Guards Brigade, 16th-5th Royal Lancers, Royal Sussex Regiment, R.A.S.C., Pioneer Corps, Canadian Army and the American Army who were the last to leave. The Barons' Hall was used for entertaining the troops with a regular programme of dances, concerts and various shows.

The major military defences were not however in the castle itself, but in the earthworks of the Little Park to the north where huge guns were placed in camouflaged redoubts, capable of firing shells directly on to the beach three or four miles away should the enemy land there. Had England been invaded, the castle would almost certainly have been destroyed because it was the front line of defence in 1940, just as it had been in the 11th century. But as it was, it escaped very lightly. A German Junkers 88 plane with live bombs was shot down overhead in August 1940 and plunged into Swanbourne Lake to the east, where its wreckage was discovered during the drought of 1989 and the bombs made safe by Royal Air Force Bomb Disposal experts; one of the 500 lb. high explosive bombs is now on display in a ground floor passage.

During the war the family retreated to a small part of the south wing, digging themselves into the Smoking Room on the ground floor to which migrated the billiard table, racing books and some comfortable chairs and sofas. Much of the rest of the castle was emptied and the contents stored.

After the war the castle was re-arranged, and re-opened to the public in 1947. The duke's youngest sister, Lady Winefride Freeman wrote a guide book for the visitors which sold for 1s. and went into several editions over the next 20 years. At the time the house was re-opened, the rooms were not all returned to their previous character. This was especially true in the east wing, which was not lived in again after the war. Much of it was used for storage while the principal rooms on the first floor were arranged as museum displays of different objects from the collection, including ceremonial robes and miniatures, along the same lines as many other 'stately homes' open to the public in the 1950s. The duke and his family lived mainly in the south wing where the rooms were re-decorated and the furniture and pictures from Norfolk House put on show. The duke and duchess had a private sitting room each opening off the big

drawing room, while the smoking room on the ground floor continued to be used as an every day dining room. The traditional house-parties, for cricket in the summer and shoots in the winter, continued to be held. The social high point in the 1950s, however, was Goodwood Week in June when The Queen and The Duke of Edinburgh came to stay in alternate years, and an annual dance was held in the Barons' Hall.

In 1959 Duke Bernard and his wife decided to move out of the castle to a smaller house built in the park, to the design of Claud Phillimore. This was intended to be used in conjunction with the castle which continued to be occupied for house-parties. The duke retained his office in the castle and Mass was still said in the chapel on a daily basis. The long-term intention then was that the new house would serve as the dower house for the duchess, there not having been one before on the Arundel Estate. The main rooms, of course, continued to be open to the public on week-days in the summer, attracting over 100,000 visitors a year in the 1960s.

When Duke Bernard died in January 1975 he was succeeded, as 17th Duke of Norfolk, by his cousin Lord Beaumont (the great-grandson of the 13th Duke). It was considered at that time giving the castle to the National Trust, but the new duke was opposed to this. Instead the family set up their own independent charitable trust for the maintenance of the castle with an endowment (produced by the renewal of the leases of the Arundel House estate in the Strand), to which the major contents of the principal rooms were transferred on a long-loan agreement, with the intention of preserving the castle and its collections for the public benefit. This was the first time that a trust arrangement of this type had been made to preserve an historic family house in England, but it has now been copied and developed by many other of the largest and most famous houses in Britain, including Chatsworth, Wilton, Grimsthorpe, Hopetoun, Harewood, Luton Hoo, and most recently by the Royal Collection.

Substantial repairs to the structure of the castle were carried out in 1976-7 under the supervision of the architects, Seeley & Paget. The roof over the Dining Room was entirely rebuilt and much of the leadwork, including that on the Barons' Hall, renewed. The interior of the castle, however, was left largely as it was when re-opened after the war,

59 *Restaurant for visitors with gothic furniture by Vernon Gibberd, 1990.*

the long-term intention being that the duke's eldest son, the Earl of Arundel would live in the castle when he was old enough and had a family of his own.

In 1987 Lord Arundel married Georgina Gore and, together with the trustees, they have carried out many alterations and improvements to the castle since then. In the state rooms open to the public several additional items, which had been in store, have been put on display and the Victorian character of the interior restored. In the Library, for instance, the carpet (made originally for Queen Victoria's visit in 1846) has been copied and relaid by Grosvenor Woodward and new crimson velvet curtains (to replace the originals eaten by moths during the Second World War) hung in the central arches; the armour has been re-arranged to re-create a Victorian Armoury, and the Billiard Room re-instated with Buckler's furniture and fittings

(removed during the war) and the walls stencilled to a medieval pattern. At the same time the arrangements for visitors have been greatly improved, with a restaurant, designed by Vernon Gibberd, on the ground floor of the west wing, and a new shop (under Lady Arundel's direction) in the Victorian kitchen.

The east wing, which had been the first part of the castle to be reconstructed by Duke Henry from 1877 onwards and which forms a self-contained house in itself, has been brought back into use and entirely re-decorated.

Despite its large size, Arundel is a very practical house. The east wing having been designed on a more intimate scale than the south front state rooms (and possessing its own entrance hall, staircases and easy access to the garden) is the most attractively habitable part of the house, especially in the summer. It made practical sense to bring all these rooms back into use again, introducing modern services and recreating some of the lost Victorian decoration and character. The east wing was originally intended to be, and is now once more, a completely self-contained family house which is capable of expanding into the Library and state rooms for Christmas, shooting parties and other large-scale entertaining as occasion requires, and as was planned in the 19th century.

The decision to restore the east wing and to move back into the castle was made by Lord and Lady Arundel after their marriage. The project required a good deal of planning and negotiation before any work could begin on site. The principal objects of the rehabilitation have been to make a modern kitchen, install a food lift (in the thickness of the outer wall), to widen some of the narrower Victorian 'arrow slit' windows, and to replan the bedroom floor with additional bathrooms and a more dramatic and spacious access corridor, as well as introducing new heating, gas and electrical services. The rooms have been totally re-decorated, and furnished from scratch, drawing on things which have been in store for many years, notably some important items from Norfolk House. The building contract began on 1 October 1990. The architect was Vernon Gibberd, and the contractors were Longleys, a national firm but based in Sussex, with very good joiners and other traditional craftsmen. The painters were Hesp and Jones of Beningbrough who had already done work for Lord and Lady Arundel at Scar House, their shooting lodge, in Arkengarthdale, Yorkshire.

David Mlinaric, the interior decorator, who has a very good eye for colour and scale, and a sympathy for Victorian buildings, has acted throughout the project as a consultant to Lady Arundel who, with her friend Lady Shelburne, has herself been responsible for much of the decoration. David Mlinaric has given much helpful advice overall, and was particularly concerned with the principal private rooms in the castle. He writes: 'Foremost in my mind was the feeling of trying to soften those strong rooms without weakening them', and he has gone to great pains over the details of upholstery and colours to achieve this aim.

With its mixture of small and larger rooms, some restored to their Victorian glory and others softened by well-chosen colours and modern comforts, the castle works surprisingly well as a family house in the 1990s. Altogether, the restoration and redecoration at Arundel marks it out as one of the most successful country house revivals of recent years. The new work has in many respects completed the scheme of reconstruction begun in the 1870s, especially as some of the decoration—such as the painting of the Billiard Room—fulfils the hitherto unexecuted intentions of Buckler and Duke Henry. Once again nearly all the family collections are suitably displayed. In addition to the Norfolk heirlooms brought from Worksop in 1838, the furnishings provided by Morant in the 1840s, and Duke Henry's discerning acquisitions of the 1880s, the house also now contains the best of the 18th-century furniture from Norfolk House in London. These accumulations form a rich and varied counterpoint to the austere grandeur of the Victorian Gothic architecture. The rooms in the castle have never looked better than they do today.

Tour of the Castle

The Victorian house has a U-shaped plan of three wings built within the 12th-century curtain wall. All three ranges present a uniform, somewhat austere face to the quadrangle with smooth ashlar elevations of Doulting and Whitby stone, 13th-century-style windows and crenellated parapets. In fact these ranges are the product of two distinct building contracts. The east wing, on the left, was reconstructed by C. A. Buckler between 1877 and 1882. The quadrangle elevation of the south wing and the whole of the west wing, on the right, date from 1890-8 (though designed ten years earlier). Beneath part of the grass lawn in the quadrangle is the fire tank, an underground reservoir for emergencies.

The east wing was planned to be, and is now again, the private family home (and retains the shell of the Elizabethan Long Gallery); the south wing incorporates the walls of Henry II's residence, and contains the state rooms intended for large-scale 19th-century entertaining; while the west wing is the more 'public' side of the house with the Catholic chapel and the Barons' Hall, and the former servants' hall and steward's room on the ground floor (now converted to an attractive restaurant for visitors, with modern gothic furniture designed by Vernon Gibberd). The original Victorian plan was devised to be flexible and so has continued both to serve its original purposes and to adapt to wider uses over time. The south wing is still the setting for formal entertaining when not open to the public, while the Barons' Hall has proved ideal for a range of events including concerts in August, during the Arundel Festival, and opera in the autumn. Mass is said regularly in the Chapel which is also used for baptisms, first communions and other family services.

The Stone Hall

The public entrance is on the west side of the quadrangle through the Stone Hall. This is a small vaulted undercroft, lined with mahogany mid-18th century-hall chairs and a Regency regulator clock from Norfolk House in London. A flight of stone stairs leads up to the principal floor and the circuit of the main rooms. There is a deliberate contrast between this undemonstrative approach and the breathtaking scale and quality of the rooms to which it gives access.

60   Stone Hall with mahogany hall chairs, 1750, from Norfolk House

The Armoury

Just as the Sculpture Gallery was an essential ingredient of the larger Georgian country house, so the armoury was an important feature of the great Victorian house, and an arrangement of arms became in many ways the equivalent and successor to a collection of busts and statues. This reflects a change of taste from 18th-century neo-classical ideals, which aimed at recreating the aura of Augustan Rome on British soil, to the romantic, medievalising evocation of the Gothic period which is the dominant strand in Victorian architecture.

The taste for displaying armour in interiors, though associated with the Victorians, can be traced back in England to the 18th century. Horace Walpole in his attempt to recreate the 'true rust of the Barons' Wars' at Strawberry Hill bought arms and armour to decorate the rooms. And in the late 18th century some old family collections of arms were rearranged and displayed to emphasise the antiquity of houses like Cotehele in Cornwall, where the armour on the hall walls survives to this day in the places where it was hung in the 1790s.

It was really from the 1820s onwards, however, that armour was popularised and made fashionable in English interiors. A key figure was Sir Samuel Rush Meyrick. In the 1820s he advised his friend Sir Walter Scott on the acquisition and display of arms and armour at Abbotsford, Scott's new house. Meyrick also sorted and rearranged the royal collections of armour in the Tower of London and at Windsor Castle for George IV. His approach was both historical and ornamental and he devised ways of displaying armour in the form of whole standing figures, like the classical marble statues in a Georgian house, or as decorative wall trophies.

Meyrick's influence was very extensive. Through his scholarly publications, such as the three volume *Critical Inquiry into Antient Armour* published in 1823, he helped to increase an understanding and appreciation of armour. His advice was much sought

on the subject, not only by collectors and architects but also by artists and stage designers. He himself formed the finest private collection of armour in Europe which he displayed in his new house, Goodrich Court in Herefordshire. This was designed 'in the style of Edward II' by Edward Blore and built in 1828. Meyrick opened it to the public and this helped further to popularise a taste for armour, as did the engravings of the house published in J. Skelton and S. Meyrick's *Engraved Illustrations of Antient Arms and Armour* in 1830.

Meyrick's collection was dispersed later in the 19th century and Goodrich Court has now been demolished. Many other great English assemblages of armour have also been dispersed: notably those from Wilton House and Parham Park. But one or two survive, of which that at Arundel is among the best. It was rearranged in the present room at the north end of the Barons' Hall in 1989 with the assistance of the Royal Armouries. The aim has been to recreate the decorative and didactic effect

61 *The armour was collected by the 15th Duke.*

of a characteristic Victorian armoury, with stands of pole arms, trophies of swords, and full suits of armour. The collection at Arundel is a comparatively late one, having been formed in the 1880s by the 15th Duke of Norfolk with the advice of Charles Davis, a Bond Street dealer who bid on the Duke's behalf at Christies and elsewhere and also negotiated some purchases on the continent between 1882 and 1898. The overall quality of the collection is high, including many fine examples from the Brett Collection, an earlier 19th-century armoury dispersed in the 1880s.

Armour

Pole Arms

South Wall (beginning on the right of the entrance)

1. Spear		17th-cent. Staff-Sergeant's leading staff.
2. Halberd		Ceremonial. Arms of King of Savoy.
3. Partizan		(From Brett Collection)
4. Halberd		Ceremonial. Arms of King of Savoy.
5. Partizan		Late 17th-cent.

East Wall

1. Glaive	Late 16th-cent.
2. Ahlspeiss	Rare. South German. 15th-cent.
3. Glaive	Late 16th-cent.

Window Bay—South

1. Halberd	16th-cent. (From Brett Collection)
2. Halberd	16th-cent. (From Brett Collection)
3. Halberd	16th-cent.
4. Halberd	Austrian *c*.1540. Arms of Bishop of Salzburg.
5. Spear	Ancestor of Partizan. 16th-cent.
1. 3 grained spear	16th-cent.
2. Bill.	*c*.1500. Early. Decoration added century later.
3. Little Halberd	*c*.1610. Engraved decoration.

Window Bay—North

1. Halberd Ceremonial.	Late 16th-cent.
2. Halberd	Arms of Aragon & Castile *c*.1540-60.
3. Partizan	*c*.1520. Very grand. Engraved decoration.

North Wall

1. Winged Partizan	16th-cent.
2. Winged Spear	16th-cent.
3. Partizan	Late 17th-cent.

North Wall—Centre

1. Partizan	Made for the Noble Guard of Augustus the Strong of Saxony for his
2. Partizan	Coronation as King of Poland. (Arms of Poland & Lithuania)
1. Halberd	*c*.1680-1700. Ceremonial.
2. Partizan	Late 17th-cent.
3. Halberd Ornamental.	Dutch, early 17th-cent.
1. Spear	North Indian. Iron. 17th-cent. A pair with 3.

2. 3 grained Spear	Late 16th-cent.
3. Spear	North Indian. Iron. 17th-cent. A pair with 1.

West Wall

1. Partizan	Late 17th-cent. Arms of the Gonzaga, Dukes of Mantua.
2. Halberd	A curiosity (?)
3. Partizan	Engraved with double-headed eagle. Used at wedding of Maria Theresa of Austria in 1742.
1. Halberd	Late 16th-cent. (From Brett Collection)
2. Halberd	Flemish. Late 15th-cent.
3. Halberd	Late 16th-cent. Straight-edged blade.

South Wall

1. Bill	16th-cent. Italian.
2. Winged Spear	Early 16th-cent. Italian.
3. Winged Spear	Late 15th-cent.
1. Partizan	Ceremonial. Dragon & mask ornaments. 18th-cent. Pair with 3.
2. Winged Partizan	16th-cent. Etched decoration.
3. Partizan Ceremonial.	Dragon & mask ornaments. 18th-cent. Pair with 1.

Sword Boards in Alcove
(to the right of entrance)

South

1. Hunting Sword or hanger, English, 18th-cent. Silver handle and 'Green Man Mask', London 1740/1. Older blade inscribed *Hounsloe me Fecit*.
2. Officer's Sword. Light Infantry. 19th-cent.
3. Officer's Sword. Boat-shaped hilt. 19th-cent.
4. Officer's Sword. Sussex Yeomanry. Scabbard with arms of 15th Duke of Norfolk. 19th-cent.
5. Officer's Sword. Boat-shaped hilt. 19th-cent.
6. Officer's Sword. By Johnston of St James's Street.
7. Brass-mounted cutlass. *c*.1800.

On the south jamb of the alcove is a rare German early 17th-century broad sword for fencing.

North

1. Hunting knife *c*.1730. Medusa's head on hilt guard. Horn handle.
2. French Empire Presentation Sword. Early 19th-cent.
3. Page's Sword. Early 19th-cent. Horse's head handle. By C. Herbert, London.
4. 1820s Officer's Dress Sabre by Prosser. Stirrup handle, embossed with oak leaves.
5. Gold-mounted officer's sabre, mid-19th cent. 14th Duke's.
6. German 19th-cent.
7. Robe Sword worn by 13th Duke at George IV's Coronation.
8. Mourning Sword (English) *c*.1770.

Above the east door to the Chapel gallery are four fencing foils (with their original buttons—a rare survival). They are late 18th- or early 19th-century, as illustrated in Rowlandson's *Henry Angelo's School of Fence, 1791.* Klingertal mark.

The trophy in the middle of North Wall

In the centre is a 19th-century electro-type copy of the shield of Charles V in the Royal Armoury in Madrid.

8 Scottish Regimental basket hilted backswords. 18th-cent.

5 modern & 19th-cent. court swords with gilt brass handles. French officer's sword with chiselled and gilt handle, c.1730.

3 19th-cent. officers' swords (Sussex Yeomanry).

2 17th-cent. style swords.

Underneath hangs the so-called Flodden Sword. (The real Flodden sword taken from the body of the Scottish King James IV was placed on permanent loan at the College of Arms in London by the 6th Duke of Norfolk. It is still there.) This is a composite piece—18th-cent. French officer's blade: Guard c.1630, Swedish: Pommel, Swiss early 16th-cent.

Big Glass Case on the West Wall

A.
1. Hunting Crossbow, German. Inlaid stock. Initialled & dated R.O. 1644.
2. Turkish sword. Gold etched blade. 18th-cent. (c.1760-90)
3. Silver mounted scabbard to 2.
4. Turkish sword & silver mounted scabbard. 18th-cent.
5. Italian sword. Gilt edged blade. Late 15th-cent. Later bronze and pearl hilt.
6. Short Sword. Composite. 17th-cent. pommel.
7. Officer's Sword. c.1620, English.
8. Spanish cup-hilted rapier. One of a pair. Dated 1796.

B.
1.-5. German Wheel-lock sporting guns with inlaid stocks. 17th- & 18th-cents.
6. Lock Carbine. Turkish. 18th-cent. Gilt etched and coral decoration.
7. Pistol with wooden butt. Early 19th-cent.
8. Pair of Scottish flintlock pistols with steel butts.
9. Ottoman Yataghan.

C.
1. Hunting Crossbow. German. 17th-cent. Inlaid stock.
2. Sword—17th-cent. type?
3. Rare 16th-cent. rapier. English. Hilt of chiselled iron.
4. Fake 16th-cent. German-type sword?
5. Short sword. Shell guard hilt. Venetian.
6. Spanish cup-hilted rapier. One of a pair. 1796.
7. Cup-hilt rapier. Hilt overlaid with silver decorations. English c.1610. Spanish blade inscribed *Juan Martin Fecit, Toledo.*

Above the case are three Hunting Crossbows. 17th-cent. German or Flemish. The English medieval iron arrow heads were discovered around the castle during the Victorian reconstruction and repairs.

Leather Shield. 17th-cent., painted with Diana the Huntress. Japanese for the European market. (Similar to one in the Ashmolean Museum, Oxford, Tradescant Collection.) Bought in 1882 at Robinson & Fisher's Sale Room.

Swords in the Window Bay

On the South Wall
Four 16th-cent. two-hander ceremonial swords (for carrying in processions). From the Brett Collection.

On the North Wall
Two-handed sword with hilt of chiselled steel. German, early 16th-cent. The broad two-edged blade is inscribed with 5 whirling rosettes and stamped with twig marks near the guard.

On the North Wall, middle bay
Chinese execution sword. (Not quite right but it makes a good story!)

North Wall, on the pier to the left of the Window Alcove
Mongley. Large two-edged sword, probably English work of early 14th cent. Bladesmith's mark of a cross within a shield. (Traditionally said to have belonged to the legendary hero Bevis of Hampton.) This is the one object in the armoury which has been at Arundel since at least the 18th century and is a very important piece.

Fire Arms

Below the Trophy in the centre of the North Wall
2 gun rests. 17th-cent. The coloured one, Indian.

On the fireplace canopy, from top to bottom
Powder casque made out of buffalo horn. 19th-cent.
8 bayonets. Mid-19th-cent. arranged in a circular trophy.
Left: Revolving Flintlock 'Wender' Fowling piece. German 1730.
Right: Continental percussion musket. 19th-cent.
Below: lee-Speed B.S.A. bolt action rifle. 19th-cent.
Bottom: Belgian sporting gun. Carved stock. c.1840.

Over the doors
Over east Chapel door (North Wall)
Blunderbuss. Early 19th-cent. By Young.
Blunderbuss. Early 19th-cent. By Young.

Over West Chapel Door
Three percussion carbines by Wilkinson. Mid-19th-cent.

Over the Tower Door (West Wall)
Two percussion muskets. By Lacy & Co., London. Mid-19th-cent.

Over West Barons' Hall Passage Entrance (South Wall)
Two double-barrelled shot guns by Wilkinson. Mid-19th-cent.

On either side of the fireplace
Pair of bronze cannon with the arms of Portugal, c.1700.

Armour

On the ceiling beam corbels, North Wall
4 light cavalry harquebusiers' helmets. Mid-17th-cent. From the English Civil War. (Brett Collection)

In Window Bay
Flemish Siege helmet, c.1610.
Coat of chain mail. Ovoid section links. Possibly Ottoman c.1500.

Suits of Armour
(Starting with North Wall, right of Chapel door, clockwise round the room)

1. Helmet, Dutch *c*.1610; Breastplate, German, 1530; Thighpieces Spanish/Flemish 16th-cent.; the rest 19th-cent.
2. Largely 19th-cent. fake; Gorget late-16th-cent.

South Wall

3. 'Maximilian Armour' 1510-30, German; Gorget, Breastplate, Pauldrons, Right Arm, Tassets, Cuishes. (Feet & helmet 19th-cent.) This is the best suit.
4. Helmet Dutch, *c*.1630; Gauntlets, Dutch, *c*.1620; Backplate English, 1660; Left Elbow Italian, *c*.1550. (Breastplate, arms & legs 19th-cent.).

On the ledge of the Alcove to the right of the entrance
Helmet and Breast and Back plates, Household Cavalry. English c. 1840. The uniform of the 14th Duke of Norfolk. Saddle. English late 15th-cent. This is a highly important, indeed unique example —the most important piece of armour at Arundel.

The Chapel

The foundation stone of the chapel was laid by the Archbishop of Southwark at a simple ceremony in 1894 and it was completed in 1898. This is the finest of Buckler's interiors at the castle and was intended to be a demonstration of the family's strong Catholicism. It is a masterpiece of Victorian craftsmanship and its noble, scholarly architecture bears comparison with the work of Pearson at Truro Cathedral or in some of his grandest estate churches like Wentworth in Yorkshire. The aim was to create a harmonious ensemble which would recall Henry III's Lady Chapel at Westminster Abbey (demolished in the early 16th century to make way for Henry VII's Chapel). Thus there is only an aisle on one side, just as the Westminster Lady Chapel is known to have had, and a polygonal apse. The sources of all the details, here as throughout the castle, are impeccably mid-13th-century, drawn especially from Westminster Abbey which provided the source for the carved angels with thuribles in the spandrels of the aisle and the Purbeck marble columns, and the Angel Choir of Lincoln Cathedral which supplied the inspiration for the especially lavish stiff-leaf carving, and the musical angels behind the altar. Every surface is covered with ornament, but such is the control and power of the design that it does not seem excessive. There is enormous variety in the detail which only becomes apparent with careful study. The carved diaper decoration in the wall arcade of the chancel, for instance, is of two different patterns

Furniture

Catherine of Braganza's Travelling Trunk
Leather 17th-century, the exterior brass-studded with crown and monogram. The interior finely tooled and gilt like contemporary book binding. Probably English. Formerly an heirloom at Alton Towers, Staffordshire. This was bequeathed to the Norfolk family by the 17th and last Catholic Earl of Shrewsbury in 1856.

Central Table
This and the following items were bought in the 1880s by the 15th Duke. The polygonal top inlaid with ivory is magnificent 16th-century Florentine work and depicts the arms of the Medici. The base is 19th-century.

Set of 4 Italian 'Savonarola' chairs
19th-cent. in 16th-cent. style. Ebonised and inlaid with ivory, partie and contre-partie. A similar chair in walnut with ivory intarsia decoration.

Pair of oak sgabelli
Italian 17th-cent.

and includes the Fitzalan oak leaves. Round the bottom arcade of the chapel the capitals of the columns are different in each arch as is the scrollwork in the spandrels. All the mouldings of the ribs and arches are embellished with dogtooth and the vault is given a lively polychrome character by alternate stripes of white chalk and creamy Painswick stone. The floor, like the columns, is of polished Purbeck marble. The Purbeck quarry, in Dorset, was specially re-opened in the 1870s to provide marble for G.E. Street's Eldon memorial church at Kingston in Dorset (1873-80). Duke Henry must have bought his Purbeck marble then, just at the beginning of his building campaign, because by the time the chapel was built in the 1890s the quarry had closed again. There was not enough Purbeck marble to do the entire job and so the shafts of the staircase arcade leading to the tribune at the back of the chapel are not of Purbeck but polished Derbyshire marble which contains larger and more obvious fossils than does Purbeck with its small, tight grain.

The stone carving is of very high quality throughout, as is demonstrated by the exceptionally deep undercutting of the stiff-leaf ornament on the Purbeck corbels of the tribune and by the seven stone bosses down the centre of the vault. These depict the life of Our Lady (to whom the chapel is dedicated), namely, from the back of the chapel to the altar: The Immaculate Conception, The Annunciation (the pot of lilies in the centre

62 *The altar, from the tribune.*

63 *Stained-glass window by Hardman.*

was copied by Buckler from a medieval original at New College, Oxford), The Nativity, The Marriage at Cana, Our Lady at the Foot of the Cross, The Assumption, and The Coronation of the Virgin in Heaven (over the altar).

The finest feature of the chapel is the stained glass which was supplied by John Hardman & Co of Birmingham and was made under the supervision of Dunstan Powell (Pugin's son-in-law). Like the bosses it mainly depicts scenes from the life of Our Lady, and its rich dark colours and strong design with roundels outlined by thick metal cames is based on the early glass at Canterbury Cathedral. The subjects of the windows are as follows (the wording is that of Hardman's original):

Windows

Five Windows in Chancel (starting from the top of each window)

1. Appearance of Our Blessed Lord to Our Blessed Lady after The Resurrection.
   Pieta.
2. Saints of the Old Testament: Adam, Eve, David, Abraham, Jacob.
   Saints: Peter, Andrew, James the Less, Matthew, Matthias.
3. The Coronation of Our Blessed Lady.
   The Assumption: Our Lady leaves St Thomas her girdle.
4. Saints of the New Testament: Joseph, Anne, Elizabeth, John, John the Baptist.
   Saints: James, John, Philip, Simeon, Jude, Bartholomew.
5. The Crucifixion.
   Carriage of the Cross.

(Small panels depict Companions of Our Lady: St Joseph, St Elizabeth, Joachim, St Anne, St John, St Simeon.)

Four Windows in Nave—Life of Our Blessed Lady

1. Miracle at Cana
   Chastity
   Finding in the Temple
   Humility
   Flight into Egypt
2. Adoration of the Magi
   David Presentation in the Temple
   Isaiah
   The Nativity
3. The Visitation
   Miriam Judith
   The Annunciation
   Deborah Esther
   The Espousals
4. The Blessed Virgin Mary presented in the temple
   The Fall
   The Birth of Our Blessed Lady
   The Creation of Eve
   Meeting at Golden Gate

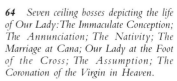

64 *Seven ceiling bosses depicting the life of Our Lady: The Immaculate Conception; The Annunciation; The Nativity; The Marriage at Cana; Our Lady at the Foot of the Cross; The Assumption; The Coronation of the Virgin in Heaven.*

Two windows on gospel side
Both depict Sibyl

Two windows in the Tribune
1. Sancta dei Genetrix
    Gideon and the Fleece
    Mater Christi
    Moses and the burning bush
    Mater Castissima
2. Mater Amabilis
    Esther interceeds for her people
    Mater Creatoris
    Judith cuts off the head of Holofernes
    Mater Salvatoris

Two windows in Staircase
1. Our Blessed Lord enthroned
    Our Blessed Lady St Agnes
    St Dorothea   St Lucy
    St Cecilia   St Barbara
    St Ursula   St Catharine
    St Etheldreda   St Margaret
    Text: 'After her shall virgins be brought to the King'.
2. The Madonna enthroned
    Saints who have been champions of the Blessed Virgin:
    Bernard, Bonaventura, Dominick, Francis, Alphonsus Liguori.
    The Immaculate Conception
    St John writing the description of the Glorious Woman in the Apocalypse

65   *Carved angels behind the altar.*

66   *The tribune, with Hardman's electroliers above.*

Hardmans also supplied the architectural metalwork in the chapel, including the iron floor grilles for the central heating, the gilt brass *repoussée* door, inlaid with rock crystals, of the tabernacle on the altar (1898) and the pair of ingeniously designed wrought-iron electroliers at the back of the chapel over the tribune.

Works of Art

Paintings

Triptych
Workshop of Pieter Cocke van Aelst. *c.*1500. 41 in. x 28 in. (Wings 41 in. x 12 in.) The central panel is the Adoration of the Magi flanked by the Adoration of the Shepherds and the Circumcision. Bought at the Beresford Hope Sale at Christies in 1886.

Double sided panel
School of Antwerp. 16th-cent. 40 in. x 21 in. Verso: Mass of St Gregory. Recto: Garden of Gethsemane.

Two side panels
From a triptych. South German. 16th-cent. 1. Recto: St James and St Bartholomew. St Francis and St Dominic, Verso. 2. St Dominic and St Bernard, Recto. Two Kings Verso. Bought at the Beresford Hope sale in 1886.

Carvings and Sculpture

The Risen Christ
Flemish 17th-cent. Carved wood, near life-size.

Marble panel of the Virgin and Child
In the Renaissance manner. 19th-cent. Florentine.

White marble bust of *Pope Pius IX* by Pietro Tenerani, Rome 1860.

Pair of statues of *St Joseph and Our Lady*. Polychrome and gilt terracotta. 19th-cent. Calissi, Toulouse.
Triptych of wood and ivory inlaid with mother of pearl and tortoiseshell, containing coloured Italian waxes depicting the Passion, Death and Resurrection of Our Lord. Turin, early 18th-cent. By Jean François Cuenot. (Signed *Canot fecit*.)

There are many other smaller objects in the chapel, many of which were wedding presents to the 15th Duke from clergy and nuns.

Silver and Metalware

High Altar
Crucifix. Wood with silver mounts. 18th-cent. German.
Set of four altar vases by Charles Kandler made for 8th Duke of Norfolk, 1730.
6 Sheffield Plate column candlesticks *c.*1790.
Gothic Silver Sanctuary lamp by E. Krall, 1905. A gift to the chapel from Gwendolen Duchess of Norfolk following her marriage.

Lady Altar
Statue of Our Lady, a replica of that on the Immaculate Conception column in the Piazza di Spagna, Rome. A wedding present from Pope Pius IX to the 15th Duke of Norfolk in 1878.
6 candlesticks by William Penstone *c.*1715.
Wrought iron candle stand. Spanish 16th-cent.

St Joseph's Altar
Statue of St Joseph. Italian 17th-cent. Bought by Duke Henry from Mr Bickerstaff-Drew, an army chaplain.
6 candlesticks by John Martin Stocker 1710, engraved with the sacred monogram IHS and the Norfolk crest and coronet.

The Barons' Hall

This vast room, begun in 1893 and completed in 1898, occupies the site of the medieval hall of the Fitzalan Earls of Arundel as well as that built by the 11th Duke of Norfolk but left incomplete on his death in 1815. It is much larger than either of those, but perpetuates the name of its Georgian predecessor. Of all the interiors at Arundel, it is the one which today perhaps best demonstrates the architectural ideas and taste of the 15th Duke of Norfolk, for not only does the design survive unaltered, but most of the furniture and some of the pictures were acquired by him in the 1880s and remain where he placed them. The room is 133 ft. long, 37 ft. wide and 50 ft. high. The hammerbeam roof is of oak grown on the estate. Buckler based his design, which was the result of ten years' gestation, on a range of original examples including the great hammerbeam roof of Westminster Hall in London. The moulding of the beams is derived from several sources such as the roofs at Penshurst Place in Kent and the Worcester Guesten Hall. Many other features of the room are also derived directly from medieval sources, French as well as English. The windows on the courtyard side, for instance, copy those in the great hall at Winchester built by Henry III, while the two huge hooded chimneypieces of Painswick stone (not a matching pair; there are differences in the carving) and the iron 'curtain cranes' are based on the publications of the French 19th-century antiquarian and architect Viollet-le-Duc who restored Notre Dame in Paris and the town of Carcassonne as well as rebuilding the huge *château* of Pierrefonds for Napoleon III. Buckler paid considerable attention to the details of the room, providing full-scale drawings of such items as the heraldic firedogs, the gothic picture hooks and the hinges and handles of the doors. The iron curtain cranes were made by Messrs Potter but the other metalwork in the room, as well as the richly coloured stained glass, was supplied between 1894 and 1898 by Hardman, Powell & Co. of Birmingham, like most of the architectural metalwork in the castle.

The stained glass in the windows is perhaps the most distinguished feature of the hall. It was designed by Buckler, incorporating the ideas of the duke himself, and is a record of family history. On the courtyard side there is heraldry, with the arms of all the owners of Arundel Castle from Roger de Montgomery (posthumous, as heraldry did not emerge in Europe till after his death) down to the 15th Duke of Norfolk. On the fireplace side the windows are devoted to the Albini and Fitzalan Earls of Arundel with notable scenes from their lives chosen from Canon Tierney's early 19th-century history of Arundel Castle and its owners. (For details see p.76.) The heraldic rose window in the north gable of the hall is particularly handsome with shields showing the principal Norfolk quarterings: Howard, Brotherton, Warenne and Fitzalan. Facing it in the south gable are three pointed lancets containing portraits of the 15th Duke of Norfolk and his first wife Flora, in heraldic tabards, kneeling on either side of Our Lady of Lourdes. This is an early example of the depiction of Our Lady of Lourdes in English iconography and a tribute from the duke and duchess who had a special devotion to her; they used to visit Lourdes every year in the hope that a miracle would cure their invalid son Philip who had been born blind and epileptic.

The original under-floor heating system for this room is still in working order and comprises an ingenious arrangement of heated pipes through which air is passed and warmed before coming up through the brass grilles set into the oak floor boards. Like all the late 19th-century central heating at Arundel this was devised by James Slater of Holborn, 'the gas and hot water engineer' who had been employed under Buckler's direction as early at 1879 to devise the 'most efficient warming apparatus' for the castle, as well as the system of electric bells for summoning servants. Buckler himself designed the 'heating coils', handsome polished gunmetal radiators to be found all over the castle. Buckler also experimented with various designs for the electric light fittings in here, but they all proved unsatisfactory and the present efficient and tactful lighting was designed, using recessed spotlights in the roof and picture lights, by the present Earl of Rosebery *c.*1960.

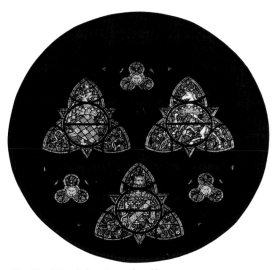

68 *Heraldic window in north gable.*

Furniture

The Barons' Hall contains the best private collection of 16th-century continental furniture in England, with an excellent series of carved oak and walnut tables, cabinets and coffers. Very little English furniture of this date has survived. Duke Henry therefore instructed his agent Charles Davis, a Bond Street dealer, to buy French, German and Flemish furniture of the type listed in the 16th-century Arundel inventory. It is a tribute to Davis's judgement, taste (and honesty) that most of what he acquired is still considered to be good by modern experts and very little of it has turned out to be fake. The Augsburg Cabinet was acquired at Christies in October 1883 for £105, and the finely carved French (Lyons) cabinet (and other pieces) at Christies in July 1884 for £525. Between 1883 and 1898 Duke Henry spent substantial sums on the purchase of furniture and objects for Arundel. Davis's account for 1883 came to £6,717 and this was exceeded in subsequent years. In 1886, for instance, the duke spent £1,310 12s. 0d. at the Beresford Hope Sale alone. The principal items are:

Screens End
German walnut chest. Finely carved with allegorical figures and heads. Nuremberg, *c.*1600).

67 *(left) Barons' Hall looking south.*

Window side
Three Italian walnut late 16th-century centre tables on elaborate carved trestle supports
French walnut late 16th-century architectural cabinet with panelled doors and incised strapwork decoration.
French walnut 16th-century cabinet with architectural decoration and two allegorical figures painted in grisaille on copper in arched panels with the triumph of Virtue over Vice.
The set of 10 George II gilt gesso armchairs have the original floral *grospoint* needlework. These chairs, which are attributed to Giles Grendey, were made for the 8th Duke and were in the Drawing Room at Arundel in 1777.

Fireplace Side
French late 16th-century cabinet decorated with Ionic columns and strapwork decoration on an open base, the decoration based on the engravings of Ducerceau.
Walnut French cabinet *c.*1600 (Lyons School) decorated with allegorical figures and inlaid with ivory. On an open base with term legs and central support carved as Janus.
Travelling writing cabinet made in Augsburg for the Spanish market. Scroll marquetry and parquetry of dyed sycamore. The arms on the front are those of the founders of the Greyfriars at Valladolid, the family of Solis Sodeno. Mid-16th-cent.
French walnut cabinet *c.*1600, the doors with incised strapwork and carved heads.
The large elm 19th-century table was formerly in the Servants' Hall.
The sedan chair is mid-18th-century and comes from Norfolk House.
The set of four gilt-framed Venetian arm chairs date from *c.*1740.
The larger of the two sleighs is German 18th-century; the smaller is a child's sleigh, Dutch, early 19th-century.

69 *Detail of fire dogs, part of Buckler's 'pack of dogs'.*

70   The Earl of Surrey defending his allegiance, by Mather Brown.

Paintings hanging on the lower walls

Triptych of the Life of the Virgin
Spanish School, *c.*1500. 38 in. x 28 in. (wings 38 in. x 11 in.). Oil on panel. The central panel shows the Madonna enthroned, with the Annunciation and the Assumption on the wings. Bought by the 15th Duke of Norfolk at the Beresford Hope Sale, Christies, May 1886.

Altarpiece of the Nativity with patron saints
Marco Palmezzano (Forli). 15th-century. 104 in. x 80 in. Oil on panel. Signed on the piece of paper lying on the ground. The saints are St Francis, St John the Baptist, St Bernard, St Jerome, St Barbara.

Cardinal Edward Howard (1829-1892)
Julian Story, signed and dated 1884. Oil on canvas 53.5 in. x 39.25 in. Painted in Rome. The Cardinal, a cousin of the Dukes of Norfolk, was Archpriest of St Peter's. Story was an American artist resident in Italy, educated at Eton and Oxford and the son of the sculptor William Waldo Story.

Charles I (1600-1649)
Anthony Van Dyck. Oil on canvas. 38.5 in. x 32 in. The prime version of this portrait which relates to the triple portrait at Windsor. At Worksop in 1777. (Miniature copy by Henry Bone, 1824.) (Cleaned by Hayman & Pugh, 1774.)

The Earl of Surrey explaining his loyalty before Henry VII
Mather Brown, 1797. 77 in. x 150 in. Oil on canvas. This large and colourful canvas was commissioned by the 11th Duke of Norfolk for Arundel Castle as part of an intended series devoted to family history. Dorinda Evans, Mather Brown (1982)

Cardinal Newman (1801-90) John Everett Millais. 47 in. x 37 in. Oil on canvas. Signed and dated 1881. Bought by the 15th Duke of Norfolk after a Catholic subscription to present it to the National Portrait Gallery had failed. (Transferred to the N.P.G., 1976.) Exhibited Royal Academy 1882 and N.P.G. 1990.

Pair of Imaginary landscapes with huntsmen
Jacques D'Artois. 67 in. x 96 in. Oil on canvas. Signed 'D'Artois'. These good, large Flemish landscapes were acquired by the 9th Duke and brought to Arundel from Worksop; they were in the Dining Room in 1846.

Historical Portraits round the upper level

Charles, 2nd Duke of Grafton (1683-1757)
J.B. Van Loo. Oil on canvas. 93 in. x 57 in. Norfolk frame carved by J.A. Cuenot. In Garter Robes. A good version of the original at Euston. He was Lord Chamberlain. Bought after 1834. Probably by 15th Duke.

Ludovic Stewart, 2nd Duke of Lennox and 1st Duke of Richmond (1574-1624)
Daniel Mytens. Oil on canvas. Norfolk frame. Versions of the portrait (without the archery scene in the background) are in the Royal Collection, in that of the Earl of Radnor at Longford, and at Petworth. Painted in 1623, the year he was created Duke of Richmond. In the collection before 1777 (where called 'a Fitzalan Earl of Arundel'). Sir Oliver Millar considers this to be a good, possibly autograph version.

7th Duke of Norfolk (1654-1701)
Simon Verelst. Oil on canvas. Norfolk frame. It was while painting a pendant to this of the Duchess (now at Drayton) that Verelst uncovered evidence of her liaison with John Germaine, leading to her divorce from the duke. At Worksop in 1777 (when thought to be Lord Thomas Howard of Worksop).

Lord Maltravers (1538-1557)
English School. Posthumous. Mid-16th-century. Oil on canvas. Probably painted for Lord Lumley. Inscribed 'Harry Fitzalleyne, the Count Mautravers eldest sonne to the Lord Harry Erle of Arundel deceased the yeare of our Lord God MDLVI being of age not fully XIX yeares'. In collection before 1777.

3rd Duke of Norfolk (1473-1554)
Mytens, after Holbein. Early 17th-cent. Oil on canvas. Probably painted for the Collector Earl. The attribution to Mytens was first made by Sir Oliver Millar. Inscribed: 'Thomas Duke off Norfolk Marshall and Treasurer off Inglonde the LXVI yere of his age'. Provenance: Bought by 15th Duke of Norfolk from Colnaghi, March 1887.

Henry Frederick, Earl of Arundel (1608-1652)
English School 18th-century, after Mytens. Oil on canvas. Norfolk frame. Previously called 'Lord Lumley'.

Cardinal Philip Howard of Norfolk (1629-1694)
Andrea Casali (signed), *c.*1750. Oil on canvas. Castle Howard frame with Dacre shells. Painted posthumously for the Earl of Carlisle. At Castle Howard in 1834. Given to 15th Duke of Norfolk by 9th Earl of Carlisle. Philip, the younger brother of the 5th and 6th Dukes, was Almoner to Catherine of Braganza and head of the English Dominicans. Sir Oliver Millar considered that this may be based on the head and shoulders painted by Michael Wright in Rome.

Queen Mary of Modena (1658-1715)
Sir Godfrey Kneller. Oil on canvas. At Arundel Castle 1777. Sir Oliver Millar considers this to be slightly better than James II.

King James II (1633-1701)
Sir Godfrey Kneller. Oil on canvas. At Arundel Castle 1777. Sir Oliver Millar considers this is probably an original of *c.*1685-7. Not in very good condition but signs of original quality.

Thomas Osborne, 1st Duke of Leeds (1631-1713)
J. Kerseboom (signed) 1705. Oil on canvas. A duplicate

71 *Spanish leather case, 17th cent. for a portable altar.*

to that formerly in the collection of the Duke of Leeds which is dated 1704. In Garter robes.

Unknown Man in Garter Robes
English School, late 17th-cent. Oil on canvas. Once thought to be the Duke of Monmouth, but not him. Bought after 1834, probably by 15th Duke of Norfolk.

Lord Howard of Effingham (1536-1624)
Studio of Mytens. Oil on canvas. Norfolk frame. A version of that in the National Maritime Museum (formerly at Gorhambury) which was painted in 1620. In the collection at Worksop in 1777. In poor condition. Possibly reduced all round. Cleaned by Hayman & Pugh 1774. Bibliography: Roy Strong, *Tudor & Jacobean Portraits*, p.319.

Tapestries

The two large tapestries hanging facing each other high up at either end of the hall are Gobelins from the *Nouvelle Indes* series, woven under Neilson's direction *c.*1750. They were commissioned directly from the factory for the Great Room at Norfolk House by the 9th Duchess, and cost £9 a yard. These two panels are *Le Chameau et L'Éléphant* (a composite weaving of two of the original cartoons) and *La Négresse portée dans un hamac*. They are based on paintings by Albert van der Eeckhout and Jan Post given by Prince Maurice of Nassau to Louis XIV; the animals in the cartoons were later repainted by Desportes. They record flora and fauna in the Dutch colonies.

Windows—Chronological Scenes

A.

Battle of Hastings, 1066
King Rufus spends Easter at Arundel, 1097
Forces of Henry I besiege Arundel
Stephen arrives with his forces but on Adeliza appealing
to his chivalry he allows Empress Maud to leave

B.

1st Earl, William D'Albini goes on a mission from Henry
II to Pope Alexander III, 1164
3rd Earl, William D'Albini swears on behalf of the King
loyalty to the Magna Carta, 1215
3rd Earl, William D'Albini renders homage to the young
King Henry III, 1216
3rd Earl, Richard Fitz-Alan at the Siege of Caerlavarock,
1300
3rd Earl, Richard Fitz-Alan builds the outer gate-way
and the Chapel of St Martin, 1295
3rd Earl, William D'Albini departs for the Holy Land,
1218

C.

4th Earl, Edmund Fitz-Alan entertains Edward I at
Arundel, 1302
4th Earl, Edmund keeps his vigil of knighthood in
Westminster Abbey with the young prince, 1306
5th Earl, Richard Fitz-Alan drives the French ships from
the Channel, 1339
6th Earl, Richard Fitz-Alan gains a victory over the French,
Spanish and Flemish ships, 1387
5th Earl, Richard Fitz-Alan appointed to take charge of
the government during the king's absence, 1355
5th Earl, Richard Fitz-Alan rescues the Black Prince at
Crecy, 1346

D.

6th Earl, Richard Fitz-Alan founds the college and hospital
at Arundel, 1380
6th Earl, veneration paid at the tomb of Earl Richard,
1397
7th Earl, Thomas Fitz-Alan leading his men at the Bridge
of St Cloud, 1411
14th Earl, Henry victorious at the Siege of Boulogne,
1544
11th Earl, William Fitz-Alan confers knighthood on
Richmond (afterwards Henry VII), 1485
Thomas Fitz-Alan at the Siege of Harfleur, 1415

E.

Saint Philip walking up and down gallery at Arundel
wishes to become a Catholic, 1583
Saint Philip cuts his inscription on dungeon wall, 1557
Saint Philip's death, 1595
4th Earl, Dukedom restored by Charles II, 1660
3rd Earl, Earl Henry Frederick fights for the king at the
Siege of Banbury, 1643
2nd Earl, Destruction of Castle by Parliamentary troops
under Walter Waller, 3rd siege, 1644

Heraldry

North side bay
Early owners of Arundel and Albini marriages
King Henry I; Adeliza of Louvain; Albini; Hilary; Blundesville (Azure 6 garbs or oswestry); Fitzalan (ancient).

Fitzalan marriages
Verdon; Mortimer; Saluzzo (Clun); Warenne; Earl of
Lancaster; Bohun.

Warenne marriages
Talvare (Roger de Montgomery); Earl Marshal (William
Marshall, Earl of Pembroke, Henry III); Le Brune; de
Vere; Fitzalan; Arundel and Surrey.

Mowbray marriages
Mowbray (ancient); Mowbray; Gournay; Gant;
Beauchamp of Bedford, Clare.

South side bay
Mowbray marriages
Braose; Edmund, Earl of Lancaster; Segrave; Thomas de
Brotherton, son of Edward I; Mowbray and Fitzalan;
Robert Howard and Mowbray.

Howard marriages
Howard-Germand; Howard-Fitton; Howard-Cornwall;
Howard-Scales; Howard-Dubois; Howard-Tendring.

Howard marriages
Howard-Mowbray; John, Duke of Norfolk-Molins;
Thomas, 2nd Duke of Norfolk-Tilney; Thomas, 3rd Duke
of Norfolk-Stafford; Henry, Earl of Surrey-de Vere;
Thomas, 4th Duke of Norfolk-Fitzalan

Howard marriages
Philip, 13th Earl of Arundel-Dacre; Thomas, 14th Earl of
Arundel-Talbot; Henry Frederick, 15th Earl of Arundel-
Stuart (d'Aubigny); Ld. Bernard Howard-Tattershall;
Bernard Howard of Glossop-Roper; Henry Howard of
Sheffield-Molyneux.

Bernard, 12th Duke of Norfolk-Belasyse; Henry, 13th
Duke of Norfolk-Granville; Henry, 14th Duke of Norfolk-
Lyons; Henry, 15th Duke of Norfolk-Hastings; Duke of
Norfolk; Earl of Arundel and Surrey.

The Picture Gallery

This was added by the 8th Duke *c.*1718 to improve the communications between the principal rooms on the south front. Reconstructed and lengthened by the 11th Duke in the 1790s, its present appearance dates from a hundred years later when it was redesigned by C.A. Buckler who faced the walls with Painswick stone, introduced a low vaulted ceiling and altered the windows (introducing heraldic glass) at either end in 1890-1. The exaggerated proportions or the room derive from the fact that while it is 192 ft. long it is only 11 ft. wide and 13 ft. high. In the 15th Duke's time this immensely long vista was lined with elaborate continental cabinets, arms and armour. The present more Georgian arrangement dates from after the Second World War when the house was re-opened to the public in 1947. At that time

Lavinia Duchess of Norfolk re-constituted the south front rooms to incorporate the furniture and paintings which had been brought from Norfolk House in 1938 and stored during the military occupation of the castle.

There are three different sets of chairs. At the west end is a group of Chippendale ribbon back mahogany dining chairs. They are based on an engraving in the third edition of Chippendale's *Director* (1762), and display a very high standard of workmanship. In the central section of the gallery is a set of early 18th-century gilt gesso armchairs with lions' paw feet and contemporary needlework covers. These were almost certainly made for the 8th Duke and were already in this gallery in the inventory of 1777. At the far end is a French 19th-century set of chairs in the Louis XIII manner,

72   *Picture Gallery looking east.*

73 The 3rd Duke of Norfolk, *after Holbein.*

74 *Needlework covered chair c.1730.*

covered with genuine 17th-century embroidered upholstery which, no doubt, they were made to display.

The various coffers and chests form part of the 15th Duke's purchases and include an English 16th-century marquetry 'Nonsuch' chest, and an Italian 15th-century travelling altar. The most impressive pieces, however, are the gilt pier tables with eye-catching tops of pinky-orange Sicilian jasper, on either side of the door to the Drawing Room. These were made for the Great Room at Norfolk House in 1750, their frames designed by G.B. Borra and carved by J.A. Cuenot, while the Jasper slabs were supplied by the architect James Paine in 1768 presumably to replace something less good.

The white marble busts all on gray marble pedestals were commissioned mainly by the 14th Duke of Norfolk, and are of his family; they comprise:

Matthew Noble	Bust of Admiral Lord Lyons, 1856
J. Francis	Statue of the Duke of Sutherland, 1842
Pietro Tenerani(?)	Bust of Pope Leo XIII (Not a member of the family!)
J. Francis	Bust of Charlotte Duchess of Norfolk, 1845
J. Francis	Bust of Henry Charles, 13th Duke of Norfolk, 1845
Matthew Noble	Statue of Admiral Lord Lyons, 1856 (a modello for his monument in St Paul's Cathedral)
Joseph Gott	Bust of an Unknown man. Rome, 1827
J. Francis	Bust of Bernard, 12th Duke of Norfolk, 1842
J. Francis	Bust of Lord Bernard Howard, 1847
Matthew Noble	Bust of the Earl of Ellesmere, 1857 (the brother of Duchess Charlotte)

The busts of King Charles I (1636) and his nephew Prince Charles Louis, Count Palatine of the Rhine (1637) are by François Dieussart, a sculptor of French extraction who trained under Bernini in Rome and was brought to England by the Collector Earl of Arundel in the 1630s; he commissioned these two works. (Busts of Lord Arundel himself and Prince Rupert, the brother of Charles Louis, by Dieussart are among the Arundel Marbles in the Ashmolean at Oxford.) These sculptures are the principal survivals of the Collector Earl's collection now at Arundel and form a notable landmark in the history of English artistic patronage. Bibliog. David Howarth, *Lord Arundel and his Circle* (1985), pp. 161-4.

Family Portraits

(Beginning to the right of the door from the Barons' Hall and working from west to east)
Man called Henry Frederick, 15th Earl of Arundel (1608-1652)

75 *English 16th-century marquetry chest.*

School of Van Dyck or Sir Anthony Van Dyck. Oil on canvas. 28 in. x 22 in. Probably not Henry Frederick. Bought after 1834. Exhibited Royal Academy, 1900.

Thomas, 14th Earl of Arundel (1585-1646)
School of Van Dyck. Oil on canvas. 28.25 in. x 24.25 in. A version of the Van Dyck of the Earl and his Grandson in a painted oval. This may have been in the collection before 1777.

Earl of Surrey (1517-1547)
18th-cent. copy after J. Belkamp *c.*1770. Oil on canvas 29.5 in. x 24.5 in. Norfolk frame. Probably a copy of a miniature portrait. cf. Portrait at Knole. Exhibited: Tudor Exhibition, New Gallery, 1890. At Worksop, 1777.

Saint Philip Howard, 13th Earl of Arundel (1557-1595)
George Gower (attributed). Oil on canvas. 18.5 in. x 14.5 in. Lumley Collection (cartellino in top right hand corner). Northwick Park Collection. Bought by Bernard, 16th Duke of Norfolk. Inscribed 'Ao Ae. 18' and 'Philippe ... Duke ...'. Bibliography: Lumley Inventory. Roy Strong, *Connoisseur* (March 1978), p. 195.

Henry Fitzalan, 12th Earl of Arundel (1512-1579/80)
John Bettes I (attributed). Oil on panel. 16 in. x 11.5 in. Norfolk frame. Inscribed: 'A. DNI 1558'. 'Ae Suae. 56.' The age is wrong—he was 46 in 1558. Bibliography: Roy Strong, *Connoisseur* (March 1978) p. 196. Exhibited Tudor Exhibition, New Gallery, 1890. There is another version at Petworth, and a copy at Sledmere. In the collection before 1777.

Henry Fitzalan, Lord Maltravers (1538-1557)
John Bettes I (attributed). Oil on panel. 34.5 in. x 28.375 in. Bibliography: Roy Strong, *Connoisseur* (March 1978), p. 197. Exhibited: Tudor Exhibition, New Gallery, 1890. In collection before 1777 at Worksop. Cleaned by Hayman & Pugh, 1774.

John, 1st Duke of Norfolk (1430-1485)
English, late 16th-cent. Oil on panel. 29.25 in. x 24 in. Norfolk frame. Inscribed: 'Jon Howard, the first Duke of Norfolk of that name'. Formerly in the Lumley Collection (cartellino in top right hand corner) and probably painted for John, Lord Lumley in late 16th century. Thereafter acquired by the 14th Earl of Arundel and by descent. Bibliography: Lumley Inventory 1590. Roy Strong, *Connoisseur* (March 1978), p. 194. Cleaned by Hayman & Pugh, 1774. Exhibited: Tudor Exhibition, New Gallery, 1890. National Portrait Gallery, 1973. At Worksop 1777.

Thomas, 2nd Duke of Norfolk (1443-1524)
English early 16th-cent. Oil on panel. 29 in. x 24.5 in. A contemporary portrait and the oldest in the collection. Inscribed 'Thomas Howard Dux Norff. obit Ao dm 1524'. This is almost certainly the portrait recorded in the Lumley Inventory. Exhibited: Tudor Exhibition, New Gallery 1890. Manchester 1897. Bibliography: Lumley Inventory 1590. Roy Strong, *Connoisseur* (March 1978), p. 194. Bought after 1834. Formerly at Greystoke.

Thomas, 3rd Duke of Norfolk (1473-1554)
After Holbein (English 16th-cent.). Oil on panel. 31.25 in. x 23 in. Norfolk frame. A studio copy of the original. There is another Arundel version in East Wing Hall. See also the versions at Windsor and Castle Howard. Inscribed: 'Thomas Duke of Norfolk Marshall and Treasurer off Inglonde. The LXVI Yere of his Age.' Cleaned by Hayman & Pugh, 1774. At Worksop 1777.

Thomas, 4th Duke of Norfolk (1538-1572)
English School late 18th-cent. Oil on canvas. 57.5 in. x 45 in. An 18th-cent. ancestor painting possibly based on a contemporary miniature or engraving. Painted between 1777 and 1827 (copy by Bone). Probably for the 11th Duke of Norfolk.

76 *Ceiling boss carved with heraldic lion.*

77 *Doors to Barons' Hall with elaborate hinges.*

Anne Somerset, 1st wife of 6th Duke of Norfolk (1631-1662)
J.M. Wright. Oil on canvas. 26.25 in. x 23.5 in. Norfolk
frame. There is a three-quarter length version of this
portrait, and also a pendant portrait of the duke, at
Badminton. The attribution is Sir Oliver Millar's. At
Worksop 1777.

Henry, 6th Duke of Norfolk (1628-1684)
Sir Peter Lely. Oil on canvas. 88.5 in. x 53 in. Signed
and dated 1677. It is rare for a portrait by Lely to be
signed and dated (Sir Oliver Millar). cf. copy in Victoria
Room and the head and shoulders variant on East
Staircase. The portrait was painted to mark Henry's
accession to the dukedom. Exhibited: National Portrait
Gallery 1978-9. Bibliography: Oliver Millar, *Sir Peter
Lely* (NPG 1978) pp. 68-9. Collins Baker II p. 129.
Beckett, No. 384. At Worksop 1777. Cleaned by Hayman
& Pugh, 1774.

Henry, 7th Duke of Norfolk (1655-1701)
English School 17th-cent. Kneller? Oil on canvas. 49 in.
x 39 in. Shows blistering and other traces of fire damage
so may have been rescued from the fire at Worksop in
1761. At Worksop 1834.

Jane Bickerton, 2nd wife of Henry 6th Duke of Norfolk (d.1693)
Sir Peter Lely. Oil on canvas. 88.5 in. x 53 in. Signed and
dated 1677. There is a good version, head only, formerly
at Corby Castle (and also of the duke). The flowers were
painted by a specialist assistant. These two portraits are
excellent examples of Lely's late manner. Exhibited:
Canada 1980. National Portrait Gallery 1978/9. Swagger
Portrait Exhibition, Tate Gallery 1992. Bibliography:
Oliver Millar, *Sir Peter Lely* (NPG 1978), pp. 68-9. Collins
Baker II p. 129. Beckett No. 385. Whinney & Millar pp.
175-6. At Worksop 1777. Cleaned by Hayman & Pugh
1774. Cleaned by Clare Wilkins, 1980.

78 *The 6th Duchess by Lely.*

79 *The Poet Earl of Surrey, showing his royal ancestry.*

Thomas, 8th Duke of Norfolk (1683–1732)
R. van Bleeck. Oil on canvas. 48 in. x 37 in. Van Bleeck
specialised in portraits of recusants. Note the little gold
cross on the duke's fob.

Mary Blount, wife of Edward 9th Duke of Norfolk (1702–
1773)
John Vanderbank. Oil on canvas. 92.5 in. x 56.5 in. Norfolk
frame. signed and dated 'Jn Vanderbank Fecit 1737'. At
Worksop 1777.

Edward, 9th Duke of Norfolk (1686–1777)
John Vanderbank. Oil on canvas. 92.5 in. x 56.5 in. Norfolk
frame. Signed and dated 'Jn Vanderbank Fecit 1737'. At
Worksop 1777.

Henry, Earl of Surrey (1517–1547)
North Italian School. Early 17th-cent. Oil on canvas. 86
in. x 85 in. Inscribed: 'Anno.Dñ . 1546. Aetatis.Sue.29'.
'Sat Super Est'. Painted for the 14th Earl of Arundel in
the early 17th century as part of a record of family history.
The allegorical figures holding shields depict the Earl of
Surrey's royal descent through his father and mother. The
architectural frame *en grisaille* may have been designed by
Inigo Jones. (Drapery added to figures in 19th century.)
Exhibited: Manchester 1965. Tate Gallery 1969. National

80   *Bust of Charles I by François Dieussart.*

81   *Bust of Charles Louis, Count Palatine of the Rhine, made
for the Collector Earl by François Dieussart.*

Portrait Gallery 1976. Bibliography: Roy Strong, *English Icon* (1969), p. 72. Roy Strong, *Connoisseur* (March 1978), pp. 199-200. At Norfolk House 1777. This portrait was bought at the Stafford House sale by Robert Walpole and given to the 9th Duke of Norfolk. Then by descent. (Transferred to National Portrait Gallery 1976.) Cleaned by Hayman & Pugh, 1774.

Charlotte, wife of 13th Duke of Norfolk (1788-1870)
Sir Thomas Lawrence. Oil on canvas. 29.25 in. x 24.25 in. Bibliography: Kenneth Garlick, *Lawrence*.

Katherine Brockholes, wife of 10th Duke of Norfolk (1718-1784)
English School 18th-cent. Oil on canvas. 92 in. x 56 in. Her hand rests on a copy of her husband's *Anecdotes of the Howard Family*.

Charles, 10th Duke of Norfolk (1720-1786)
English School 18th-cent. Oil on canvas. 92 in. x 56 in. Henry Howard in 1834 said by Opie but this is doubtful.

Elizabeth Leveson-Gower, wife of 2nd Marquess of Westminster (1797-1891)
Sir Thomas Lawrence. Oil on canvas. 29.5 in. x 24.5 in. She was the sister of Charlotte, wife of 13th Duke of Norfolk. A replica of that in the Sutherland Collection at Dunrobin Castle. Exhibited: Royal Academy 1818. Bibliography: Kenneth Garlick, *Lawrence*.

Charles, 11th Duke of Norfolk (1746-1815)
Sir Thomas Lawrence. Oil on canvas. 49 in. x 39 in. This is the best of the Lawrences at Arundel. Exhibited at the Royal Academy 1799. Bibliography: Kenneth Garlick, *Lawrence*.

Bernard Edward, 12th Duke of Norfolk (1756-1842)
H.W. Pickersgill. Oil on canvas. 35.5 in. x 27 in. A reduced version of the Catholic Emancipation portrait in the Dining Room.

Augusta Mary Minna Catherine Lyons, wife of 14th Duke of Norfolk (1821-1886)
English School, 19th-cent. Oil on canvas. 35.5 in. x 27.5 in.

Henry, 15th Duke of Norfolk (1847-1917)
Philip de Laszlo. Oil on canvas. 47.5 in. x 33.25 in.

Bernard, 16th Duke of Norfolk (1908-1975)
A.C. Davidson-Houston. Oil on canvas. This portrait is posthumous and was done from a photograph. It is a replica of one in the possession of Lavinia Duchess of Norfolk.

Henry Charles, 13th Duke of Norfolk (1791-1856)
Sir George Hayter. Oil on canvas. 105.5 in. x 69 in. Framed by Morant 1845. The Duke is depicted in Westminster Abbey in his robes as a 'supporter of the king's train' at the Coronation of George IV. Exhibited: Royal Academy 1824. At Worksop in 1834. At Arundel by 1846. Cleaned by Clare Wilkins, 1982.

Henry Granville, 14th Duke of Norfolk (1815-1860)
John Partridge. Oil on canvas. 92 in. x 56.5 in. This picture was painted in 1862 and cost £414. 15s. 0d. Bibliography: Accounts in the Arundel Archives A1974. Cleaned by Clare Wilkins, 1982.

Anne Constable-Maxwell, wife of 17th Duke of Norfolk (b. 1927)
June Mendoza. Oil on canvas. 1979.

Miles, 17th Duke of Norfolk (b. 1915)
June Mendoza. Oil on canvas. 1979.

The Dining Room

The lack of an exact medieval source for a Victorian state dining room spurred Buckler to heights of invention and this is one of his most pure and original architectural creations, bearing little resemblance to a gothic great hall which would have been the nearest equivalent. (Arundel already had a super-version of one of those.) The slightly ecclesiastical air is, however, not coincidental, for part of the shell of this room is Henry II's chapel added to the castle *c.*1180; it had been resuscitated as the private Catholic chapel for the 8th and 9th Dukes in the 18th century. The 11th Duke (who conformed to the Established Church) moved the chapel and the priest out of the castle to the old College buildings next to the Fitzalan Chapel in

the 1790s, and transformed the space into a large dining room with gothick mahogany fittings, of which the set of four handsome serving tables survives. The 15th Duke in the 1880s thought of restoring the room as the chapel (and moving the Dining Room to the north side of the Picture Gallery) but changed his mind and built the present larger and grander chapel in the west wing instead. The three tall lancet windows, however, survived from the 1885 chapel design as the duke liked them. The room is 60 ft. long, 23 ft. wide and 34 ft. high. The oak wainscotted Barrel-section ceiling is carried on eight stone springer arches reminiscent of the work of Norman Shaw. The capitals supporting these have good stiff-leaf carving

82 *Dining Room.*

by Rattee & Kett's craftsmen. The chimneypiece on the other hand is devoid of carved ornament and incorporated into the boldly modelled wall surfaces. The interior of the fireplace is lined with heraldic tiles designed by Buckler and made by Minton; the three alternating patterns incorporate the Mowbray silver lion rampant, the Fitzalan gold lion rampant and the Howard cross crosslets fitchée. Buckler also designed the iron firedogs, curtain cranes and the pendant electroliers, all made by Hardman, Powell & Co in 1898. Duke Henry personally approved the drawings for all these: 'I like the suggestion of [the] chains for [the] electric lights', he wrote to Buckler in 1898. Even the smallest details of the design were considered by the duke who took a close interest in the whole rebuilding project over the quarter of a century that it took to complete. The trophies of 17th-century pole arms and breast plates on the walls are as arranged in the 1890s and form part of the architectural decoration of the room.

Furniture

The set of seat furniture round the room was made for the ground floor drawing room at Norfolk House in 1750 by Joseph Metcalfe. The needlework covers (dated between 1752 and 1762) were made by the 9th Duchess of Norfolk and her helpers. They incorporate scenes from Aesop's fables. (When the room is not in use these are protected by modern linen case covers with the Norfolk monogram and coronet embroidered by the Royal School of Needlework in 1991.)

The four neo-classical Dining Room urns and pedestals of inlaid satinwood dating from *c.*1780 were possibly made for the 10th Duke. The painted decoration was added in the 19th century to make them look more 'Sheraton'. They are a fine example of a short-lived furnishing convention, which combined fashionable decoration with practical use. The pedestals were hot-plates, metal-lined with a tray for hot charcoal at the bottom and racks for

83 Dining Room through the door from the gallery.

keeping the plates warm. The urns originally had taps and linings so that they could be filled with water for rinsing the plates between courses. Silver plates were used for dining in 18th-century ducal houses and porcelain only for dessert.

The magnificent French clock in a Boulle case on the side table was made in the early 18th century by Jérôme Martinot; it is surmounted by gilt bronze figures of Minerva and the three fates. This was one of Duke Henry's purchases. The pair of turquoise blue vases on carved stone brackets flanking the fireplace are 18th-century Chinese.

The blue and gold dessert service displayed around the room is Derby, *c*.1800.

Dining Room plate (silver gilt)

On Dumbwaiters
Two Wine Coolers Made by Paul de Lamerie and Paul Crespin 1727, magnificent examples of French *Régence* decoration. They are almost identical in design to the Chesterfield wine cooler in the V & A. They are the earliest 18th-century English silver to incorporate large areas of figurative chasing and are among the most elaborate examples of Huguenot silver to survive.

On Table
Punch Bowl By Benjamin Pyne, 1706. Made for the 8th Duke of Norfolk (listed in the inventory of 1777). Embellished with the Norfolk lion crest on top of the lid.

Two Coasters By Paul Storr, 1835. Made for the 12th Duke of Norfolk. An unusual Heraldry-inspired design made up of N monograms supported by the Norfolk lion and the Arundel horse.

Two Candelabra Candlesticks 1815 by Jonathan Hayne, Branches and feet by Paul Storr, 1832. Made for the 12th Duke of Norfolk.

Six Salt Cellars Rococo design with mermaid feet and shell decoration. By Charles Kandler, 1732. Made for the 8th Duke of Norfolk.

Four dessert dishes By Benjamin Pyne, 1723.

On Side-table
Sheffield Freedom Casket Presented to the 15th Duke of Norfolk, 1897. He was the first Lord Mayor and first Freeman of the City of Sheffield.

Dining Room plate (gold)

Coronation Cups presented to the Earl Marshal
George II Thomas Farrer, 1727.
George III Gurney & Cooke, 1761.
George IV Designed by Thomas Willement, in the 'Old English Manner', 1822. Made by Philip Rundell of Rundell & Brydges. With a silver-gilt stand to match.
George V Garrard 1911
George VI Garrard 1932 Queen Elizabeth II 1953

The Earl Marshal's baton. Gold with black enamel tips and the Royal arms at one end and the Norfolk arms on the other. The design of the Earl Marshal's baton was laid down by Richard II in the 14th century. This example was made in 1837. The Earl Marshal carries the baton on official occasions such as the State Opening of Parliament.

A Presentation baton. The stem enamelled in red, green and white with a heraldic dragon among red and white roses, a ducal coronet at one end and the Norfolk arms at the other. By Robert Garrard, 1877. Presented by the College of Arms to the 15th Duke of Norfolk on his marriage to Lady Flora Abney-Hastings, 21 November 1877.

Mary Queen of Scots Relics

The Gold Cross and Rosary Beads of Mary Queen of Scots
Mary Queen of Scots is traditionally said to have bequeathed to Anne Dacre, Countess of Arundel, the rosary beads which she had with her at the moment of her execution at Fotheringhay. There is no mention of this in Mary's will, but accounts of her last day describe how she distributed the contents of her wardrobe, including clothes and jewels, to her attendants, and also charged Pierre Gorion, her pharmacist, to distribute certain

84 *Rosary beads of Mary Queen of Scots.*

85 *Pearl necklace of Mary Queen of Scots.*

mementoes to her friends. These would have included the rosary to Lady Arundel. In the contemporary description of her execution it is stated that the chief executioner tried to claim as his perquisite the gold cross she was wearing, but that Jane Kennedy, one of the ladies in waiting, snatched it away and Mary said to him 'Friend, let her have it: she will give you more than its value in money'. There is no documentary proof that the rosary was sent to Lady Arundel, but there is no reason to doubt it. It is known to have been in the possession of her son, Thomas the 'Collector' Earl of Arundel, in the early 17th century.

The rosary then passed by descent in the Howard family. The 11th Duke of Norfolk allowed his cousin and executor Henry Howard of Corby (who was interested in the family history and relics) to have it on his death in 1815, but it was re-acquired from Corby by the 15th Duke later in the 19th century.

[Henry Howard, *Memorials of the Howard Family* (1834), section IX. British Museum: Harleian MS Vol. I, Article 290, p. 196.]

The wooden pomander rosary beads
These have a relic of the true cross and are also traditionally said to have belonged to Mary Queen of Scots, but they are not documented.

Pearl necklace
This is formed of River of Tay pearls separated by gold *fleurs de lys* recalling that Mary was also Queen of France. This was bought in London by the 15th Duke of Norfolk as a wedding present for Flora, his first wife, in 1877.

The small gold cross which once belonged to Mary Queen of Scots
This was bought by Mary Howard, wife of Lord Thomas Howard of Worksop and mother of the 8th and 9th Dukes of Norfolk. The following note is preserved in the archives: 'This Gold Cross was Queen Mary of Scots and in those troublesome times she gave it to the Abott of Wesminster and by what meanes I know not it came into ye hands of Mr. Loyeck ye monk and I bought it by chance and by these letters it is mine I gave the mony for it in ye year 1696. (signed) Mary Howard of Worksop'

86 *Silver gilt wine cooler by Paul de Lamerie and Paul Crespin, 1727.*

87 *George IV's coronation cup designed by Thomas Willement, made by Rundell & Brydges.*

The Abbot of Westminster was Abbot Fecken-ham, who was appointed Abbot when the Abbey was restored under Queen Mary Tudor. After Queen Mary Tudor's death in 1558 the Abbey was once more dissolved and Abbot Feckenham was sent to the Tower in 1560 and spent the remaining 24 years of his life either in jail or under surveillance of some kind, sometimes for example in the charge of an Anglican bishop. He could therefore have received the cross as a present from Mary Queen of Scots at any time.

Mr Loyeck ye monk was Fr. Henry Bernard Lowick, a Benedictine who was professed at Douai in 1673, in the community which the surviving monks of Westminster had founded in France. The cross was very likely held in that community. He came to London in 1685 and was in the community established by King James II at St James's Palace; he escaped to Paris in 1688, where he became sub-prior of a small monastery which was a Jacobite centre. Mary Howard of Worksop also fled to Paris after 1688 with her children, and would have known Fr. Lowick there.

Prayer Book
Illuminated 16th-century Book of Hours of the Use of Troyes. Traditionally said to have been given by Mary Queen of Scots to Lord Herries after spending her last night in Scotland at Terregles, his house in Dumfriesshire, following her defeat by the Scottish nobles at Langside. The following day she crossed the Solway to England to seek the protection of her cousin Elizabeth. This has passed by descent in the Herries family and is now the property of The Lady Herries (14th in line), eldest daughter of Bernard, 16th Duke of Norfolk.

Portraits

(clockwise from the left)
Bernard, 12th Duke of Norfolk (1765-1842)
Henry W. Pickersgill. 54 in. x 42 in. Oil on canvas. Commissioned to commemorate the passing of the Catholic Emancipation Act in 1829. The duke is painted in peer's parliamentary robes which were made specially for him to take his seat in the House of Lords consequent on the passing of the Act (and which are the same ones that the present duke wears at the State Opening of Parliament every year), with the Act and Earl Marshal's baton on the table beside him. (The silver mounted quill pen used by George IV to sign the Act is displayed in the case below; it was given to Lord Howard of Glossop, the present duke's great-grandfather.)
Henry Charles, 13th Duke of Norfolk (1791-1856)
Henry W. Pickersgill. 40 in. x 25 in. Oil on canvas.
Mary Blount, wife of Edward 9th Duke of Norfolk (1702-1773)
John Vanderbank. 1732. 44 in. x 33 in. Oil on canvas. Norfolk frame. This is a reduced version of a portrait signed and dated 1732 also in the Norfolk collection in which the floral wreath she holds is about to be placed round the neck of a tame deer.
Thomas, 14th Earl of Arundel, 'The Collector' (1585-1646)
English School. 1610. 81 in. x 45 in. Oil on canvas. Arundel frame. This is the earliest of the portraits of the Collector Earl at Arundel and shows him dressed in Greenwich armour and holding a painted wooden baton for the New Year Barriers, a tournament-type entertainment which took place at Whitehall Palace in 1610, and where he was the supporter of Henry Frederick Prince of Wales.
At Arundel in 1777 (when wrongly called 'the King of Bohemia'). Roy Strong, *Connoisseur* (March 1978).
Elizabeth, Princess Palatine of the Rhine and Queen of Bohemia, 'The Winter Queen'
Francis Miereveldt. 81 in. x 45 in. Oil on canvas. Arundel frame. Signed on the edge of the table-cloth. The Collector Earl accompanied her on her marriage procession to Heidelberg in 1612 and acted as a special ambassador on her behalf on several subsequent occasions. At Arundel in 1777.

The Drawing Room

This is the earliest of the Buckler state rooms, having been begun in 1877. It occupies the shell of Henry II's great hall. The 'best quality oak wainscot' ceiling and carved cornice were made to Buckler's design in 1879 by Rattee & Kett, being their first work at Arundel. The frieze cost £300 and the ceiling with its moulded ribs and small carved bosses £408. The frieze is a typical heraldic conceit of Buckler's (based on two days' research in the College of Arms); it shows all the quarterings brought into the Howard family through marriages to heiresses from the late 13th to the 19th centuries, the painted shields seemingly hung from a continuous carved ribbon which is pinned into place at intervals with Howard *cross crosslets fitchée*.

The arms are as follows: Fitzalan, Earl of Arundel; Howard (before 1513); Fitton; Dubois; Scales; Tendring; Mowbray; Mowbray (ancient); Gournay; Beauchamp of Bedford; Earl Marshal (William the Marshal); Warenne, Earl of Surrey; Braose; Bruce; Miles Fitzwalter, Earl of Hereford (12th century); Marshall of Rye (official coat for office of Marshal 1300); 'Strongbow' (Gilbert and Richard de Clare, Earls of Pembroke, Earls Marshal 1138-76); Clare; Segrave (ancient); Segrave; Thomas of Brotherton; Albini/Fitzalan; Fitzalan (ancient); Clun; Ufford; Brett; Blundeville, Earl of Chester; Hugh Lupus, Earl of Chester (Time of William I); De Vere; Plantagenet (Hameline), brother of Henry II, Earl of Warenne and Surrey by right of his wife;

88 *Drawing Room.*

Warenne; Woodvile; Maltravers; Tilney; De Ros
(Manners); Mowbray, Duke of Norfolk; Rochford;
Thorp; Dacre; Moulton of Gillesland; Greystoke;
Redeman (Cumberland); John of Lancaster (Baron,
1299); Botiller of Wemme; De Morvile; Ferrers of
Chartley (temp. Henry III); De Vaux of Gillesland;
Howard, Duke of Norfolk; Talbot; Talvace (Roger
de Montgomery, through his wife Mabel de
Bellême); Ancient Talbot; Comin of Badenoch;
De Valence (Earl of Pembroke); Munchensie; Le
Strange; Giffard; Clifford; Neville (differenced by
a martlet) Lord Furnival; Neville; Bulmer; De
Furnival; Lovetot; Tattershall; Molyneux; Bellasis;
Bellasyse; Butterlet; Caltoft; Barton; Lyons; Fitzalan,
Earl of Arundel.

The Painswick stone chimneypiece is an even
more swagger heraldic performance, the work of
Thomas Earp, doyen of Victorian architectural
sculptors, who charged the very modest price of
£150. It is a ducal performance in every way, the
top cresting being derived from the strawberry
leaves of a ducal coronet while more naturalistic
strawberry leaves embellish one of the capitals (the
other has Fitzalan oak leaves). Stylised strawberry

90   *Firedogs designed by C. A. Buckler, made by Hardman.*

flowers also make their appearance on the Minton
tiles in the fireplace alongside the Warenne chequers
and Howard crosses. The frieze of arms over the
fireplace comprises: Brotherton, Segrave, Mowbray,
Fitzalan, Warenne, Clun and Maltravers. The
principal armorial achievement, on the hood of
the chimneypiece, displays the arms of the 15th
Duke of Norfolk impaled with those of his first
wife Flora (Abney-Hastings).

Buckler's full-scale drawings for the lion-headed
fire dogs survive, part of a 'pack of dogs' which he
provided for the castle. They were made by
Hardmans as were the curtain cranes which support
curtains of green cut velvet to a Pugin design. The
stone-coloured walls were originally intended to
be painted in the medieval manner with a pattern
of red lines and scrolls derived from the King's
Hall in Winchester but this was never carried out
(though it provided the inspiration for the recent
decoration of the Billiard Room in the private
apartments). The picture rails were however painted
in a somewhat startling manner by Buckler with
red and white stripes like barbers' poles. The present
deployment of the furniture dates from 1947 when
the room was re-arranged to incorporate the best
things from Norfolk House, notably the set of
serving-table and two matching pier tables of
English ormolu with black Derbyshire marble tops
made in 1750 for the Dining Room. These unique
pieces have no direct equivalent in English
furniture-making. The pier tables have recently been
re-assembled (for the first time this century) with
their matching pier glasses; the gilt frames carved

89   *Chimneypiece carved by Thomas Earp, 1877.*

with vines are by J.A. Cuenot. The arm chairs
with original Soho tapestry coverings are another
of the sets provided by Joseph Metcalfe for the
ground floor rooms at Norfolk House in 1750.
The pair of gilt Italian Neo-classical tables with
green marble tops on either side of the
chimneypiece, though transferred from Norfolk
House in 1938, were in fact purchased by Duke
Henry in October 1883 for £300. The table with
the superb Florentine *pietra dura* top (under the
Mytens portraits) was also bought by him in 1883,
as also was the fine *Régence* Boulle clock by Claude
Artus, made for an admiral, hence the nautical
symbolism. The portraits in here include some of
the best in the collection; their hang pre-dates the
Victorian reconstruction, repeating that in the
drawing room at Worksop whence most of the
pictures came:

Portraits in the Drawing Room

(Beginning on the right hand wall and continuing anti-
clockwise)

*Aletheia, Countess of Arundel in the Picture Gallery at Arundel
House* (d.1654)
Daniel Mytens. Oil on canvas. 81.5 in. x 50 in. Norfolk
frame. Pair to Lord Arundel. Exhibited: Treasure Houses
of Britain, Washington, 1985. At Worksop in 1777.
(Transferred to the N.P.G. 1976.) Cleaned by Hayman &
Pugh, 1774.

*Thomas Howard, 14th Earl of Arundel, in the Sculpture Gallery
at Arundel House* (1585-1646)
Daniel Mytens. Oil on canvas. 81.5 in. x 50 in. Norfolk
frame. Painted in 1617 soon after Mytens' arrival in
England. Exhibited: Tate Gallery 1972 'Age of Charles I'.
Treasure Houses of Britain, Washington, 1985.
Bibliography: Haworth, *Lord Arundel and his Circle*, p. 57
etc. At Worksop in 1777. (Transferred to the NPG 1976.)
Cleaned by Hayman & Pugh, 1774.

Henry Frederick, 15th Earl of Arundel (1608-1652)
Anthony Van Dyck. Oil on canvas. 56 in. x 44 in. Norfolk
frame. In Armour. Inscribed: *Droit et Avant.* Acquired
between 1777 and 1834.

*Thomas Howard, 14th Earl of Arundel with his grandson Thomas,
later 5th Duke of Norfolk* (1585-1646 and 1627-1677)
Anthony Van Dyck. Oil on canvas. 56 in. x 47.25 in. This
is among Van Dyck's best English portraits and the finest
portrait now at Arundel Castle. At Norfolk House in 1777.
Exhibited at Tate 1972. N.P.G. Van Dyck exhibition 1982.

Sir Walter Pye
Anthony Van Dyck. Oil on canvas. 42 in. x 30 in. Provenance:
From Lely's collection. Bought after 1834. Bibliography:
Malcolm Rogers, *Burlington Magazine*, April 1982.

Thomas, 4th Duke of Norfolk (1538-1572)
After Hans Eworth. Oil on canvas. 84 in x 46.5 in.

Norfolk frame. 18th-century copy made presumably for
the 9th Duke after the fire at Worksop in 1761. Inscribed:
'Thomas Duke of Norfolk etcetera HE pinxit Anno
155[6]'. At Worksop in 1777. Cleaned by Hayman &
Pugh, 1774.

Mary Fitzalan, Duchess of Norfolk (1540-1557)
After Hans Eworth. Oil on canvas. 84 in. x 46.5 in.
Norfolk frame. Pair to 4th Duke. Inscribed: 'Mary, Duchess
of Norfolk etcetera, daughter and sole heiress of Henry
Fitzallan, Earl of Arundel etcetera HE pinxit anno 155[6]'.
At Worksop in 1777. Cleaned by Hayman & Pugh, 1774.

Bernard, 12th Duke of Norfolk (1765-1842)
Thomas Gainsborough. Oil on canvas. 88 in. x 54 in.
Painted in Van Dyck costume. Bibliography: Waterhouse,
Gainsborough No. 518.

Lord Thomas Howard of Worksop (1657-1689)
Sir Joshua Reynolds. Oil on canvas. 84 in. x 52 in. Norfolk
frame. A posthumous portrait of his father commissioned
by the 9th Duke after the Worksop fire in 1762. At Worksop
in 1777. Bibliography: Waterhouse *Reynolds*, p. 44.

Charles, 11th Duke of Norfolk (1746-1815)
Thomas Gainsborough. Oil on canvas. 91.5 in. x 60 in.
Painted in Van Dyck costume. Bibliography: Waterhouse,
Gainsborough, No 517. (Transferred to N.P.G., 1976.)

William Howard, Viscount Stafford (1614-1680)
After Van Dyck. Oil on canvas. 43.25 in. x 36.75 in. An
18th-cent. copy of the original in the collection of the
Marquess of Bute (Mount Stuart). At Worksop in 1777
where called *Lord Maltravers.*

91 The Collector Earl and his grandson 'Little Tom', *by
Van Dyck.*

Henry Bone Enamels

On the tables in the Drawing Room

Henry Bone perfected the technique of painting miniatures on porcelain plaques and made a career out of painting small copies of family portraits. Other groups of his work can be seen at Woburn and Kingston Lacy.

1. 'Henry Fitz-Allen—the last Earl of Arundel of that Name—Steward of the Household—Chancellor of the University of Oxford—Born 1511—died 25th Feby 1579—aged 68 years. After the original by Sir Antonio More, Arundel Castle, Duke of Norfolk' (Handwritten inscription on the back on paper. Also a printed label: Js. Anty. Molteno, Printseller, No. 20 Pall Mall.)

2. 'Lord Maltravers—the last of the Fitzallens. Painted by Henry Bone—Enamel-painter to His Majesty and Enamel-painter to His R.H. the Duke of York etc etc—after the original in the collection of His Grace the Duke of Norfolk, Norfolk House, London.' 'Feb. 7 1826. No. 15 Berners St., London.' (Handwritten on the back. Printed label of Molteno.)

3. 'Henry Howard, Earl of Surrey, from the original at Worksop Manor. "the bravest soldier, the sweetest poet and the noblest gentleman of his time". 1517-1547.' (Hand-written inscription on back.)

4. 'Thos. Howard fourth Duke of Norfolk of that name. Lieutenant in the northern counties etc etc —Earl Marshal—executed June 2d 1572. After the portrait at Worksop Manor—Duke of Norfolk.' (Handwritten on paper on the back. Molteno label.)

5. 'Philip Howard, Earl of Arundel—Died a prisoner in the Tower, 1595. Painted by Henry Bone R.A. Enamel-Painter to His Majesty and Enl—Painter to His R.H. the Duke of York etc etc after the original in the possession of the Earl of Surrey—Worksop Manor, Nottingham. No. 15 Berners St., London.' (Handwritten on paper on the back. Molteno label.)

6. 'Charles Lord Howard of Effingham, Earl of Nottingham, Lord High Admiral of England, and Commander in Chief against the Spanish Armada—Died Sept 11 1624, aged 84. After the picture in the collection of the Rt. Hon. Lord Viscount Grimston, Gorhambury, Herts.' (Printed on paper. Molteno label.)

All have engraved on the gold mount (bottom right-hand corner): 'ENAMEL H BONE R.A.'

Miniatures

The miniatures displayed in the two Victorian cases on the Italian side-tables are:

Case I

1. *Lord Bernard Fitzalan Howard* Aged 1½. Anthony Stewart. 1827.
2. *Lord Fitzalan* (later 14th Duke of Norfolk) Aged 11½. Anthony Stewart. 1827.

92 *Miniatures of Prince James 'The Old Pretender' and his sister Isabelle, by Artaud.*

3. *Lady Mary Fitzalan Howard* (later Foley) Aged 3. Anthony Stewart. 1827.
4. *Charles, 10th Duke of Norfolk* Christian Zincke.
5. *Elizabeth, Duchess of Sutherland* Henry Bone. 1826. After a miniature by Mrs. Mee. Left by the Duchess to her daughter Charlotte, wife of 13th Duke of Norfolk.
6. *Little child* (not identified).
7. *King Charles II.* English 17th cent.
8. *Mary Anne Coppinger*, 1st wife of Charles, 11th Duke of Norfolk. S. Cotes. 1768.
9. *Anne Roper*, wife of Bernard Howard. (Grandmother of 12th Duke.)
Case II
1. *Henry Charles, 13th Duke of Norfolk* Franz Weigl. 1845.

2. *Lady in Tudor dress* (unidentified)
3. *Lady Adeliza Fitzalan Howard* (later Manners). Franz Weigl. 1845.
4. *Duke of Sutherland* Henry Bone. 1820. After a portrait by Thomas Phillips. Bequeathed to his daughter Charlotte Duchess of Norfolk.
5. *King Charles II* English 17th-cent. in original frame.
6. *Queen Catherine of Braganza* English 17th-cent. in original frame.
7. *James Stuart, The Old Pretender* Jacques Antoine Artaud. *c.*1700.
8. *Isabelle Stuart, Sister of The Old Pretender* Jacques Antoine Artaud. *c.*1700.
9. *Queen Anne* Christian Richter.

The Grand Staircase

This makes deliberate contrast to the low proportions of the Picture Gallery. It is the secular equivalent of the chapel with soaring vaults of striped chalk and Painswick stone, and sumptuous embellishments of marble and crisp stone carving. The inter-mixing of religious statuary and family heraldry in this space makes it the quintessence of Victorian Arundel. The rich Early English style represents Duke Henry's personal taste. The well is a perfect square, and the steps are arranged in wide leisurely flights, as if under the crossing tower of a cathedral. The staircase balustrade is an elegant design of quatrefoils and bosses of stylised foliage. Each of these is different, some making play with the Fitzalan oak leaves. The handrail itself is of polished fossil marble, as are the slim columns supporting the under-side of the stairs. The six newels are topped off with excellently carved heraldic beasts (3 lions, a horse, a wyvern and a stag) carrying shields of the principal Norfolk quarterings: Howard, Brotherton, Fitzalan, Warenne, Fitzalan (Ancient) and Duke Henry's own quartered arms at the top encircled by the Garter and with the crossed Earl Marshal's batons behind. Looking down on either side from beneath the vault are life-size statues by Boulton of Cheltenham of St Henry and St Flora, the patron saints of the 15th Duke and his first wife, with appropriate heraldry in the flanking spandrels—the arms of the Duke of Norfolk and Earl of Arundel on one side, and the varied quarterings of the Abney-Hastings family on the other. Nor is the heraldry confined to such demonstrative displays, it

93 *Grand Staircase.*

permeates the whole design; the borders of the tall lancet windows, for instance, are in the Norfolk livery colours of red, white and gold. A statue of the Immaculate Conception is set under a tall crocketed canopy while the three carved bosses in the vault represent a nativity scene with the manger in the centre and Mary and Joseph kneeling on either side.

94 (above)   Vault over staircase.

95   Central boss with the Child Jesus.

The two Gobelins tapestries from the *Nouvelles Indes* series are part of the same set as those in the Barons' Hall and were made for the Great Room at Norfolk House *c*.1750. These two are *Le Cheval rayé et Le Combat d'animaux* (a composite weaving of two of the original cartoons) and *La Chasseur Indien*. They are based on paintings by Albert van der Eeckhout and Jan Post given by Prince Maurice of Nassau to Louis XIV, the animals later repainted by Desportes. They record indigenous flora and fauna in the Dutch colonies.

Paintings

The four portraits by Henry Smith are of the children of the 13th Duke: Lord Bernard (1825-46) who died in Egypt a few days before his 21st birthday, Lord Edward (1818-83) who was created Lord Howard of Glossop and is the great-grandfather of the present duke, Lady Mary (1822-

97) who married Lord Foley and Lady Adeliza
(1829-1904) who married Lord George John
Manners MP.

Under the stairs hangs a view of the principal
18th-century seat of the Dukes of Norfolk,
Worksop Manor in Nottinghamshire, painted by
William Hodges (1777); it shows the north front
as rebuilt by the 9th Duke and Duchess after the
1761 fire, to the design of James Paine. (It was
never completed and was sold in 1838 to the Duke
of Newcastle who demolished it.) The appearance
of Worksop before the fire is shown in the two
engravings by Nathaniel Buck (1745) hanging in
the central window embrasure.

The six high-backed marquetry chairs are early
18th-century Dutch and were acquired by Duke
Henry via Charles Davis in June 1887 for £60.
The side tables are also Dutch. On the carved
chest under the Hodges painting of Worksop Manor
is a rare 13th-century Italian crucifix of gilt copper
with enamel decorations.

96 (right)   *Newel with the Brotherton arms.*

97 (below)   *Looking down into the well.*

The Victoria Room

An outer range of bed and dressing rooms was added to the courtyard side of the south range as part of the 11th Duke's alterations *c*.1790. A suite of these was specially refurnished by the 13th Duke for Queen Victoria's visit in December 1846. The white and gold tester bed, dressing table, wash stand and other matching pieces in 'Old English' style were made by George Morant, the fashionable decorator. The visitors' book signed by the Queen and Prince Albert, and the quill they used are also on display in the bedroom. The portrait of the Queen by William Fowler was specially commissioned by the 13th Duke in 1843. Fowler advised on the frame with the crown on top.

In the adjoining dressing room are two mahogany dining chairs, also made specially by Morant for the Queen and Prince Albert, and two steel spades made by a tenant in Sheffield for the royal couple to plant oak trees in the grounds of the castle to commemorate their visit. The full-length portrait by Lowes Dickinson is of Admiral Lord Lyons, grandfather of the 15th Duke and commander-in-chief of the Mediterranean fleet for the latter (and successful) part of the Crimean War. This is a replica of the portrait which Duke Henry presented to the United Services Club.

There are also four 19th-century water colours of the Fitzalan Chapel:

Joseph Nash, *Roundheads encamped in the Fitzalan Chapel*, 1860

Frederick Nash, *Interior of the Fitzalan Chapel*, 1836

George de Paris, *Interior of the Fitzalan Chapel*, 1855

98 *Victoria Bedroom showing the furniture specially made by Morant, 1846.*

99 *Queen Victoria's homage throne used at her coronation in 1838, given by her to the Earl Marshal.*

Herbert Augustine Gribble, *Interior of the Fitzalan Chapel*, 1874

Queen Victoria's homage throne, used at her coronation in Westminster Abbey (1838) and given by her to the Duke of Norfolk, sits in an alcove just outside the dressing room door.

The Ante Library

This room, which is somewhat reminiscent of the House of Lords, survives partly as remodelled in the early 19th-century. The thin-ribbed plaster ceiling and moulded plaster cornice date from then. The elaborate Puginian chimneypiece is a very tactful insertion by the 15th Duke and C.A. Buckler; note, for instance, how the carved stonework picks up the sinuous oak leaf decoration of the cornice. It is interesting that in this room, and the Library itself, an effort was made to keep the Victorian alterations 'in keeping' by using a late-medieval Perpendicular style rather than the 'Early English' gothic preferred for the rest of the building. The heraldry emphasises the early descent of the Dukes of Norfolk. The central shield quarters Howard, Brotherton, Mowbray, Segrave, [Earl] Marshal, Braose, Fitzalan, Warenne. It is flanked to the left by the Norfolk lion holding a banner of Brotherton and, on the right, the Fitzalan horse holding a banner quartering Fitzalan and Warenne. On the left canted corner of the chimneypiece, the shields, carved as if hanging on the branches of a tree, are from top to bottom: Fitzalan, Fitzalan (ancient), Ufford, and Howard impaled with Hastings; on the right canted corner are Warenne, Clun, Maltravers, and Howard impaled with Hastings. The two 'window alcoves' were added to

100 *Ante Library chimneypiece designed by C. A. Buckler, 1877.*

101 (above)   Detail of carved doorcase to the Library.

the room in 1898 to improve the natural lighting; formerly there was only one window and the room must have been rather dark. In the 18th century this was used as the dining room.

Furniture

The four lacquer cabinets and coffer came from Worksop where in the 18th century every bed and dressing room had a piece of lacquer furniture.

The set of early 18th-century 'back stools' also came from Worksop, and like the chairs in the Picture Gallery retain good contemporary needlework.

The pair of early 18th-century rosewood commodes inlaid with ivory and mother of pearl are North Italian (Piedmont) and were an acquisition of the 15th Duke's, as was the large carved ebony cabinet in the left 'window alcove'. It is French, *c.*1650 and is in the style of the Paris cabinet-maker Jean Macé. It was acquired at the Beresford Hope sale in 1886 and cost £115.

102 (below)   *The Madagascar portrait of the Collector Earl, by Van Dyck.*

Paintings

A Gonzaga Prince
Sir Peter Paul Rubens. (Wrongly called 'Philip Earl of Arundel') Oval. Oil on canvas. This is probably a head from the great group family portrait of the Gonzaga family painted by Rubens which was cut up in the 18th century into separate portraits now scattered among several different collections.

The Madagascar Portrait of the Earl of Arundel and his wife Aletheia Talbot
Sir Anthony Van Dyck. 1635. 52 in. x 83 in. Oil on canvas. This commemorates Lord Arundel's unfulfilled scheme for colonising Madagascar (to which he points on the globe, while Lady Arundel holds navigational instruments). The paper in the foreground shows their crests: the Howard lion, Fitzalan horse and the Talbot talbot hound. In the background can be seen the 'Arundel Homer', a Greek bronze bust now in the British Museum.

Italian Nobleman
Niccolo dell'Abbate. 47 in. x 38 in. Oil on canvas. Bought in the 19th century as a portrait of the Poet Earl of Surrey which it is not, but it is nice to have it anyway!

Mary Countess of Stafford
J. Michael Wright. 23 in. x 17 in. Oil on canvas. The widow of William, Viscount Stafford, the younger son of the Collector Earl who was wrongfully executed at the time of the Titus Oates plot. His widow was created a countess for life by James II as a sort of apology. She is dressed in widow's clothes.

Gwendolen, Duchess of Norfolk
Maurice Randall. Second wife of the 15th Duke and Baroness Herries in her own right. Full length. 79 in. x 50 in. Oil on canvas.

Henry, 15th Duke of Norfolk as Lord Mayor of Sheffield
Ernest Moore. 48 in. x 39 in. Oil on canvas. Signed and dated 1897. Presented by the City of Sheffield. Duke Henry was the first Lord Mayor of Sheffield in 1897-8. The Dukes of Norfolk have been substantial landowners in Sheffield since the 17th century when that estate came to them as part of the inheritance of Aletheia Talbot. Exhibited at the Royal Academy, 1897.

The Library

This is the principal survivor of the 11th Duke's architectural work and the most immediately attractive room in the castle. It was deliberately preserved by Duke Henry as the best part of his predecessor's work. It occupies the shell of the Elizabethan Long Gallery and is 112 ft. long. It was created by the 11th Duke in 1801 to his own design and is entirely fitted out in Honduras mahogany which he bought as a shipload in the London docks. It is like being inside a large wooden model for a church. The style is freely Perpendicular and the duke's secretary, James Dallaway, claimed that it was based on St George's Chapel, Windsor. Much of the charm of the room comes from the naturalistic carving with all kinds of leaves and berries, which is the work of a father and son team, Jonathan Ritson (Senior and Junior) who came from the duke's estate at Greystoke in Cumberland. After the work at Arundel was finished, Jonathan Ritson (Junior) went on to Petworth to restore the Grinling Gibbons' carvings for Lord Egremont. (A portrait of him still hangs there.) The Perpendicular fireplace-alcoves, like chantry chapels, scooped out of the thickness of the 12th-century curtain wall, were made to Buckler's design in 1898. The brass electric light fittings (by Hardman Powell & Co.) were also added to the gallery balustrade at the same time. As in the Ante Library, Buckler's alterations here were remarkably sympathetic to the Georgian gothick.

The room was refurnished by the 13th Duke for Queen Victoria's visit in 1846, and the large set of red velvet upholstered seat furniture supplied by Morant at that time survives *in situ*. Morant also provided the table to support the circular top of micro-mosaic displaying the Norfolk arms impaled with Leveson-Gower, commissioned by the 13th Duke from the Chevalier Barberi in Rome in 1847. The original fitted carpet with its striking colours was supplied for Queen Victoria's visit and has recently been rewoven exactly to the old design by Grosvenor Woodward Ltd. The red velvet curtains in the central crossing arches have also been reinstated as shown in 19th-century photographs and water colours. The fabric is Watts' Norfolk-pattern stamped velvet as supplied to the castle in the 1880s and 1890s (Watts still has the original roller). The well-upholstered couches, sofas and armchairs, the fitted carpet and the red curtains transform the Library into a surprisingly comfortable and, for its size, intimate apartment.

As well as the Morant furniture there is much else in the Library. The celestial globe was made *c*.1770 by George Adams, mathematical instrument-maker to George III. The terrestrial globe was made to match in the early 19th century. At either end are pairs of important 17th-century cabinets acquired by Duke Henry. At the south end there are Flemish cabinets veneered in red tortoiseshell with ivory placques of hunting and battle scenes

103 *The Library looking south.*

104   *Water colour by Catherine Lyons, 1858.*

after engravings by Tempesta. These were acquired through Charles Davis in December 1883 and cost £100; a bargain. At the north end is a splendid pair of Indo-Portuguese cabinets from Goa, with ivory inlay, marquetry and carved figures. The exotic note is continued in the pair of hanging Chinese lanterns decorated with Canton enamel, dating from 1820. (There is no evidence to support the legend that these came from Brighton Pavilion.)

Many of the small religious objects dotted round the room were wedding presents to the 15th Duke. The gilded figurehead is a trophy from the Crimean War and comes from the Russian warship *Maloditz* which was burnt by the British Navy. The large silver icon is by Fabergé and was a votive offering for the birth of Bernard, late Duke of Norfolk. It was commissioned by Gwendolen Duchess of Norfolk in 1908.

Perhaps the most unusual of the many curiosities in the room is the Viking ivory horn (made from a walrus tusk, not an elephant's). It is a copy of a gold horn found in 1639 at Gallehus, near Møgeltønder, North Jutland. It was presented to the King of Denmark (Christian IV) who handed it to the Crown Prince Christian (V). The following year the Crown Prince showed it to Ole Worm (1588-1654—the father of Scandinavian pre-history) who published it: Ole Worm, *Die aureo ... Cornu* (Copenhagen, 1641). This not before the prince, Asterix-like, had had it fitted with a stopper at the mouth piece to serve as a drinking horn. In 1734, only a few paces from the find-spot of this horn was discovered its pair. Both these musical instruments are fully described and schematically illustrated in: George Stevens, *Old Northern Runic Monuments of Scandinavia and England* (Edinburgh/Copenhagen, 1884) pp. 85-9. From this work we learn that the gold originals 'wandered to the melting pot, the prey of a rascally thief, in 1802'. There is a pair of electrotype reproductions, presumably made from casts, in the National Museum, Copenhagen. But this ivory copy is probably the best record of the destroyed original.

The subjects represented on the horns show the joys of Valhalla and the agonies of Helheim

105 (above)   Miniature of the Collector Earl's family with the Pageant Shield.

106 (right)   The 16th-century Italian Pageant Shield.

107   The Norfolk Book of Hours, illuminated by Simon Bening.

respectively. These are detailed in: J.J.A Worsaae, *The Industrial Arts of Denmark* (South Kensington Museum Art Handbooks, London, 1883), pp. 54-6. The style and iconography is that of Germanic imitations of Roman gold medals of the 4th-6th century A.D.

The Pageant Shield

The Italian 16th-century pageant shield was in the collection of the Collector Earl of Arundel. It may have been given to him by Charles I and come from the gallery leading to the Tilting Yard (now Horseguards' Parade) at Whitehall Palace, which was hung by Henry VIII with a group of shields. They were given as prizes to the victors in tournaments and similar pageants. The Arundel shield is similar to the D'Este shield in the Philadelphia Museum of Art (USA) and is painted with scenes from Roman history. The artist is not known.

The large 17th-century miniature of the Earl of Arundel and his family by Philip Fruytiers records the shield when it was in the collection in the 17th century.

The Library Books

The books in here comprise about 10,000 of the total of approximately 20,000 in the castle. This is the historic nucleus of the family library. There are several other rooms in the castle fitted with book shelves and the more modern books, sets of continuing reference works and the present duke's own personal collection are kept in these. In addition there are six muniment rooms which contain the family and estate papers dating from the 13th century to the present day, making it one of the most significant private historical archives in England. The main library is essentially a 'gentleman's' library of the 18th and 19th centuries. (The great library of the 'Collector' 14th Earl of Arundel which included *in toto* the library of Pyrkheimer, a friend of Dürer, was given to the Royal Society and College of Arms by the 6th Duke in the late 17th century.) The great majority of the present books were bought by Edward, 9th Duke after the fire at Worksop in 1761 which began near the library there.

The 11th Duke also added a number of rarities, including 16th-century English printed books and pamphlets, a small but choice group of illuminated manuscripts, a First Folio of Shakespeare and many fine colour-plate volumes.

108 Central vault of carved mahogany.

109 Detail of boss under gallery.

The 15th Duke added further books, mainly on architecture or heraldry, or specially connected with the family history.

The Library today consists chiefly of books on:

Art and Architecture including all the standard 18th-century English architectural folios and the complete works of Piranesi.

Heraldry with books on Honor, Arms, Funerals, Coronations and genealogy.

History—notably early editions of Leland, Camden and Holinshed.

Botany, Horticulture and Wild Life with fine colour-plate books illustrating flowers, fruit and animals.

Literature with many complete sets of French, English and Latin classics.

Topography and Travel such as Captain Cook's *Voyages*, Dampier's *New World*, Denon's *Egypt* and a particularly strong section on Sussex.

Catholic Religion—Bibles, Missals, Recusant pamphlets and controversy, notably a collection of 114 17th-cent. works on the Jesuits and the 'Pro and Ante Popery' series covering the religious debate in the reign of James II.

They reflect the tastes and interests of particular members of the family. There is, for instance, next to no science, mathematics, modern philosophy or 'modern' literature.

Ground Floor: The South Passage, Undercroft and 'Guard Room'

The South Passage is a long corridor which runs under the Picture Gallery and shares the same dimensions. Its chief architectural interest is that the south (left-hand) wall is the original courtyard frontage of Henry II's palace of 1180. One of the original buttresses, two of the doubled splayed windows and a round arched doorway all survive

110 *(right)   Basement Passage with stored logs.*

111 *(below left)   The vaulted Boiler Room under the west wing, 1894.*

112 *(below right)   Basement Box room with travelling chests for silver supplied to the 12th Duke by Rundell & Brydges, 1820.*

113 *South Passage from the east, with arms and stags' heads.*

in good condition; the latter leads into the 12th-century undercroft which has a barrel vault of chalk blocks, which supported the floor of Henry II's great hall (now occupied by the present Drawing Room). This room was never a dungeon but was always a store-room; in the 18th century it was the castle's wine and beer cellar. The other rooms opening off this passage are all domestic offices: the china cupboard, still room, butler's pantry and so forth. Many of these have simple, stout, oak cupboards and tables designed by Buckler and made by the carpenters employed on the general building contract. Buckler also designed the wooden trolleys used for pushing heavy things along these stone passages. Nearly as much thought was given to the service side of Victorian Arundel as to the grand rooms up above. Below the south passage is a further basement passage lined with alcoves for storing the

logs which can easily be transported by lift (originally hydraulic powered, but altered to electricity in the 1930s) to the upstairs rooms when they are needed. (For winter house-parties at Arundel log fires are still lit in all the guest bedrooms.) The basement also contains the wine cellar, the old electrician's workshop, the luggage store and a huge brick vaulted boiler room, under the Barons' Hall, where small modern gas boilers (1978) have replaced the giant Victorian coal-fired boilers. The east and west wings are connected under the quadrangle by a white glazed brick subway constructed as an afterthought in 1898 at a cost of £1,651. So, there is nearly as much below ground at Arundel as on the surface.

The south passage is lined with stags' heads, cases of stuffed birds and arms and armour. The stags' heads all came from the herd of red deer

114   *Deptford chimneypiece, 16th-century.*

established in the park by the 11th Duke and kept there till the second world war. The original deer came from Badminton by canal. The barge must have looked like Noah's Ark with all the antlers bobbing around on board. The stuffed birds include several specimens of a family of American eagle owls. They were originally established in the keep by the 11th Duke, as a sign of his radical Whig sympathies with the American 'rebels' after the War of Independence. (He called the farms on his Cumberland estate after American victories and heroes: Fort Putnam, Bunkers Hill, Jefferson.) When the ivy was cleared off the keep in 1868, the owls stopped breeding, and as they died they were stuffed.

The arms and armour down here are the Arundel 'second eleven' with the plainer 16th- and 17th-century pole arms and breast plates, and also some outright fakes such as the pseudo-medieval helmets supplied by Samuel Pratt and made by Grimshaw, a well-known forger of ancient armour.

Hanging opposite the central arches into the stone-vaulted front hall (called the Guardroom by the antiquarian-minded Buckler though it never

was), is the carved 16th-century overmantel from the old admiralty office at Deptford. It has the arms of the 3rd Duke of Norfolk who was Lord High Admiral of England in the reign of Henry VIII. His nephew, Lord Howard of Effingham used the same room when as Lord High Admiral in his turn he organised the English fleet which defeated

115   *The Guard Room which serves as the front hall.*

the Spanish Armada in 1588. When the Deptford admiralty was demolished *c.*1800, this was rescued by Benjamin Tucker (Secretary to the First Lord of the Admiralty) and taken to his house in Cornwall, Trematon Castle. It was bought by Duke Henry from his descendants in 1887. The two inscribed panels (added in the early 19th century) record the exploits of Sir Edward Howard off Brest, and the two little prints depict the 'Henry Grace de Dieu' built at Erith, 1515.

The English oak furniture was bought for the 15th Duke by the architect M.E. Hadfield from 'Mr Crompton'. It came from Clayton Hall, Droylesden, Lancashire. The grained early 18th-century hall chairs with the Norfolk crest in the 'Guardroom' were already at Arundel in 1777.

THE PRIVATE APARTMENTS

(Some of these can occasionally be visited by specialist groups, and the Billiard Room is usually open on weekdays in the summer season.)

116   Billiard Room with wall stencilling devised by Lord Arundel.

The East Wing

The principal rooms on the first floor comprise the Billiard Room, opening out of the north end of the Library, the Dining Room (originally the breakfast room) and the Drawing Room. They are all strongly Victorian gothic and have large, stone, hooded chimneypieces of 'truly Early English character' for the construction of which Painswick stone 'of finest texture and palest colour' was chosen by Buckler. The fireplaces are lined with polychrome Minton tiles depicting Fitzalan Howard and Abney-Hastings heraldry. A similar theme also permeates the design of the stained glass in the windows and the wrought-iron door furniture.

The Billiard Room is of particular interest as the only room in the castle for which Buckler also designed matching Puginian Gothic furniture of

117   Detail of carving with Fitzalan horse over Library door.

118   East Dining Room with Watts wallpaper and curtains.

appropriate scale and quality. Removed during the war, this has now been repaired and reinstated; it includes a pair of high-backed oak settles which fit exactly into the space on either side of the door from the Library. These benches help to make sense of the design of this wall, with the arcaded gallery above providing an elevated viewing place for spectators. The benches were restored by John Hart, who, together with the castle's own staff, has repaired much of the furniture in the private rooms in recent years.

The billiard table itself was made by Riley Barwat Ltd. to Buckler's design and is supported on stout octagonal columns. A Puginian side table has similar octagonal legs and bears the label of Charles Nosotti, a fashionable Victorian London decorator and furniture-maker better known as a purveyor of neo-Rococo gilt and for whom, reading between the lines, Buckler had no high regard. Most spectacular of all is the electric-light fitting, a huge contraption suspended from elaborately wrought-iron chains and embellished with Norfolk lions' heads, which was made for the room in the 1890s and has now been rehung in its intended position.

A considerable improvement has been achieved in the Billiard Room by painting the walls according to an original suggestion of Buckler with lining out in red on a stone-coloured ground in the medieval manner. The masonry pattern was devised by Lord Arundel, making use of the cross

119   Door handle.

120   Wrought-iron electrolier designed by C. A. Buckler.

crosslets of the Howard arms and thus continuing the heraldic theme which is such a feature of the interior at Arundel. This introduction of colour and pattern, together with the cleaning of the stonework, has successfully restored the original character of the room and helps to bring out the high quality of the Victorian architecture. A final touch is the dark-bordered green carpet runner woven by David Luckham, who was also responsible for supervising the reweaving of the carpet in the Library next door.

The Dining Room is identical in size to the Billiard Room (27 ft. by 25 ft. sq. and 17 ft. high). Here the walls have been hung, above Buckler's polished oak dado, with a dark green and gold paper specially printed by Watts, the firm of ecclesiastical furnishers in Westminster who had provided some of the original fabrics for Arundel in the late 19th century. It is finished with a red and gold chevron patterned border. The arrangement of the curtains and valances in a matching fabric is based on a sketch design by Carr of York for curtaining the pointed arched windows at Grimston

121 *East Drawing Room.*

Garth in Yorkshire. This drapery is a swagger performance well suited to the size of the room. Both the curtains and the wallpaper are examples of the 'Malvern' pattern, a gothic design originally devised by G.F. Bodley in about 1880. It is thus perfect in both date and scale for Arundel.

The Dining Room furniture comes mainly from Norfolk House, including the large, early 19th-century mahogany table and chiffonniers in the Gillow manner. The paintings include a pair of large flower pieces signed and dated 1706 by Jan Baptiste Bosschaerts, which were originally overdoors in the Tapestry Room at Worksop Manor in Nottinghamshire. The subdued colours of the wallpaper and fabrics work particularly well at night, when the table is lit by candles and the dark greens are a good foil to the Georgian silver.

The Drawing Room, 50 ft. long, is the largest of the private apartments and is filled with light from windows down both sides, in addition to the large bay window overlooking the gardens at the north end. The summery character of this room is enhanced by the yellow glaze on the walls which,

like the Billiard Room decoration, is based on an idea in one of Buckler's letters to the 15th Duke, in which he included a batch of yellow colour samples for the 'small drawing room'.

Buckler's curtain cranes have been brought back into use with new curtains of fringed Palmeston damask. Buckler's wrought-iron electroliers, which here as elsewhere in the castle have survived intact, are gilded rather than painted black.

Much thought has been given to the arrangement and upholstery of the furniture in the Drawing Room, to create an informal and comfortable atmosphere in what used to be a somewhat gaunt and daunting room. A Victorian critic, for instance, commented that it was not 'like an ordinary boudoir'.

Some of the smaller 16th- and 17th-century family portraits have been hung in this room, such as the little-known double portrait by Mytens of the Collector Earl of Arundel and his wife, Aletheia, which was originally painted as a gift for Dudley Carleton, James I's minister in Flanders, and acquired for Arundel at the Northwick Park sale

122 Minton tiles in fireplace with Hastings heraldry.

are hung here, including a recent acquisition of the 7th Earl of Shrewsbury, from whom was inherited both Worksop (sold in 1838) and the valuable Sheffield estate.

The rest of the ground floor is occupied by cosy low-ceilinged rooms: the study, nursery day room, the small dining room and the family kitchen. The latter is commodious and comfortable, with a dining table and chairs grouped around an open fireplace at one end, while the kitchen fittings are arranged next to the Aga at the other. The new oak cupboards round the walls were designed in a light-hearted gothic manner (complete with crenellation) by Vernon Gibberd and made by Longley's joiners.

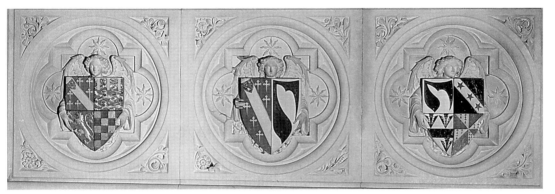

123 Carved shields in top of bay window.

in 1963. Among the furniture is a pair of superb early 18th-century looking-glasses which had additional gilt curlicues added to their frames by G.B. Borra in 1750 to fit his Italianate Rococo decoration in the state rooms at Norfolk House. Borra also designed the pair of gilt rococo pier tables (carved by Cuenot), with yellow inlaid, grey marble tops, for the First State Drawing Room at Norfolk House. A similar pair with white marble tops, from the Second State Drawing Room, has been placed in the adjoining corridor which leads to the Oak Stairs. This, the principal staircase in the east wing, is embellished at the foot with the Howard crest on the newel, for which the carver charged £3 in 1877. Both the staircase and the corridor have specially woven new Turkey runners, acquired through Keshishrian of Pimlico Road, which have strong colouring and patterns.

The Oak Stairs lead down to the stone arcaded entrance hall. More of the 16th-century portraits

124 Spiral staircase vault and newel, 1877.

The Upper Gallery

At the top of the main staircase, this passage runs the full width of the south range but is divided into three parts. The centre is faced in Painswick stone and is vaulted like the Picture Gallery below. But each of the end sections is treated differently: the western part is lined with book-cases and the eastern contains flights of stairs connecting bedrooms on different levels.

The stonework of the gallery was cleaned and the whole redecorated in 1994. In it are displayed some of the major religious paintings in the Norfolk collection.

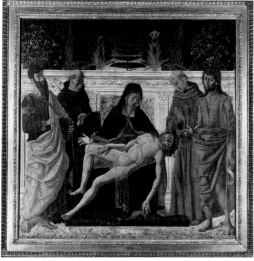

125   *Upper Gallery* Piéta *by the Master of San Miniato, 1460.*

A Pièta with Saints Bartholomew, Nicholas of Tolentino, Francis and John the Baptist
Master of San Miniato. Oil on panel. 67 in. x 70 in. Dated 1460 and inscribed with the names of the saints.

Altarpiece of Madonna and Child
Giulian Agostino. Oil on panel. 75 in. x 70 in. Signed and dated 1455. Acquired by the 15th Duke in Rome, 1878 as 'a bargain' via W.H. Manning of the Piazza di Spagna.

Two Panels with The Annunciation (Angel on one: Our Lady on the other)
Michael Packer. Oil on panel. 57 in. x 31 in.

St Michael the Archangel
School of Avignon. *c.*1450. Oil on panel. 52 in. x 29 in. This is the only work of this school in an English collection.

Pièta with St Francis and St Barbara
Umbrian School. Early 16th-cent. Oil on panel. 51 in. x 33 in. Not very good quality. Bought in Rome from a shop in the Via Sistina by W.H. Manning for the 15th Duke.

The Adoration of the Shepherds
Benedetto Gennari. Oil on canvas. 101 in. x 83 in. This historically important picture was the altarpiece painted for James II's short-lived Catholic chapel at Whitehall Palace. In the 18th-century it served the same function at Arundel. No. 106 on Gennari's list.

Small triptych
Workshop of Cornelis Cornelisz. Crucifixion. Wings: 2 female donors (Bridgettine Nuns) and St Barbara and St Apollonia. Male donor and St James. Bought by the 15th Duke from the architect J.A. Hansom.

Small triptych
French School. The Crucifixion and Fountain of Salvation. Wings: The way to Calvary and The Deposition. Recto: saints and donors.

The Bedrooms

There are about 20 principal bedrooms at Arundel. The chief guest rooms in the castle are called after the Heralds, a tradition which was initiated by the 11th Duke and which reflects the fact that the Duke of Norfolk as Earl Marshal is in charge of the College of Arms. There is a York, Chester, Lancaster, Richmond and a Marshal's Room, though the eight bedrooms along the Red Passage, over the Library are merely known as numbers: One, Two, Three, etc. These were occupied by Queen Elizabeth II as a suite when she stayed for Goodwood Week in the 1950s and 1960s. They were nearly all redesigned by C.A. Buckler between

1879 and 1882, with stone gothic chimneypieces and oak doors, in a simplified version of the architecture of the main floor of the castle. Buckler called them 'spacious rooms in 13th century style'. Originally they were decorated with Puginian fabrics from Crace, and 'hangings in medieval taste' from Helbronner of Oxford Street. But over the years these have largely given way to lighter taste. All the rooms have good Georgian furniture, accumulated family portraits, or early 19th-century water colours by Copley Fielding, Prout and their contemporaries collected by the 12th Duke of Norfolk in the 1820s and '30s.

126 *Chester Bedroom. The principal guest rooms are named after heralds.*

Arundel Park

The park, comprising an area of more than 1,000 acres, lies to the north of the castle from which it is separated by the little park, now the cricket ground, and its encircling earthworks.

It occupies some of the most beautiful downland landscape in the south of England and has long been a favourite subject for artists, particularly water-colour painters. In the Duke of Norfolk's collection alone there are paintings of scenes in the park by, or attributed to, William Daniell, Thomas Girtin, Copley Fielding, Turner and Constable.

The park was made by the 11th Duke of Norfolk as an integral part of his scheme for restoring Arundel Castle to be the principal ducal seat in the late 18th century. The old park, sometimes known as the Rewell Wood, lay to the west of the town of Arundel, completely separated from the castle. Until the late 18th century the land to the north was in different ownership and comprised rough downland used as a rabbit warren and sheep walk. In 1786 the 11th Duke of Norfolk bought 1,145 acres specially to form the new park adjoining the castle, which he enclosed and, by special Act of Parliament, added to the settled estates. (Rewell Wood was at the same time converted into the home farm.)

The enclosing of the new park sparked off a series of large-scale improvements. A three-mile stretch of the London road was diverted to its present line and the old road within the park became a private drive. At the same time the boundary wall, several miles round, was built of flint and stone and several lodges built in a castellated gothick style, of which that at Whiteways with octagonal corner turrets is the best example. The new park was also furnished with a number of decorative buildings of which a prospect tower 50 ft. high called Hiorne's Tower is the most prominent. It was designed by Francis Hiorne of Warwick in 1787 (and is a rare example of a building called after its architect). It is a good solid piece of 18th-century gothic revival architecture, triangular in plan with three octagonal corner turrets, pointed and mullioned windows and attractive chequered flintwork walls. The 11th Duke intended to use Hiorne to design a new castle at Arundel, but Hiorne died first (in 1789) and the restoration work undertaken between *c.*1794 and 1807 was done to the duke's own design. It seems likely that the duke himself was also responsible for the layout of the park with its belts and clumps of beech and other forest trees. James Dallaway in his *History of the Western Division of Sussex* in 1832 described the park as 'presenting scenes worthy and characteristic of the pencil of Claude Lorraine or of G. Smith'.

In the mid-19th century some additional lodges were built to the design of William Burn for the 13th Duke, but on the whole the park survives largely as created by the 11th Duke. Extensive restoration work and replanting has been undertaken since the great storm in 1987.

The Georgian gothic work at the castle has largely been replaced by the achievements of other architects at various dates in the 19th century, so the park is now the major contribution of the 18th century at Arundel. Together with the castle and its subsidiary buildings it forms one indivisible architectural and landscape composition which Geoffrey Jellicoe has described as being one of the 'most assured and grand' of its kind and one of the outstanding achievements of the English Picturesque. The planting of the park forms the essential background and setting to the castle, particularly as seen from the river valley, the railway or the water meadows south of the town.

The park falls into two main parts, the flat plateau to the west on which Hiorne's Tower is situated and the sweeping downland and the long shallow valley with wooded sides, to the east, stretching north from Swanbourne Lake which was originally the millpond and is of medieval origin. Near the lake is the dairy, a characteristic complex of decorative farm buildings admired by Queen Victoria on her visit to Arundel in 1846.

The park has been open to the public free since it was made except for a short time under the 13th Duke 'but the successor to that nobleman ... re-opened these pleasure paths ... observing that he delighted in seeing the public enjoy themselves in his park' (*West Sussex Gazette*, 26 September 1878), and it has been open ever since.

The principal buildings in the park are:

Hiorne's Tower Designed by Francis Hiorne of Warwick, 1787. A triangular gothic tower. Restored in 1992.

Butler's Lodge William Burn. 1850.

Whiteways Lodge *c.*1787. Probably designed by the 11th Duke of Norfolk. Gothic.

Duchess's Lodge Attributed to Robert Abraham *c.*1830. Tudor Gothic.

Swanbourne Lodge by William Burn. 1850. Tudor.

Offham Lodge by William Burn. 1850. Flint and bargeboards. Howard lion and Fitzalan horse on gateposts.

The Dairy Robert Abraham. Dated 1845. Built by 13th Duke. (By Swanbourne Lake.)

Greek 'altar' or plinth brought back by Lord Lyons from the Crimean War. (Near Hiorne's Tower.)

Index

Note: A page reference in italics indicates an illustration on that page.